towada va sohum . Family Harmony
Ta va da so hum

Praise for *In Your Elements*

" I have had the pleasure of mentoring Monica Bloom through her Ayurvedic

journey since 2010, or as she likes to put it, I have been her "teach." Monica

knows how to see things lightly with a great sense of adventure and fun

These qualities come through loud and clear, but do not let this

Still waters run deep. Monica has put in her time studying this va.

of life thoroughly. She is able to take textbook knowledge and bring

which is a skill few have. Ayurvedic practitioners will want to share th

with their clients, and students of Ayurveda will love the way she reveals the

essentials in simple and easy to assimilate ways. *In Your Elements: A Blooming*

Ayurvedic Guide to Creating Your Best Life is a unique offereing that will

entertain, but more importantly, will create enthusiastic allies for Ayurveda

as they fully participate in their healing journey."

Arun Deva
Arunachala Yoga & Ayurveda
Los Angeles, Calif.

yogarasayana.com

1

IN YOUR ELEMENTS

MONICA BLOOM

Gratitude and acknowledgments

Jessica Vellela. My little miracle partner, you are an immense blessing and addition to my world. Thank you for contributing your classical Ayurvedic knowledge and invaluable expertise. *hands at heart center*

Heidi Kraft. Thank you for inspiring these words in my soul, "I am the spark who inspires, beautifies and makes Ayurveda simple for the sake of making millions of people happy." YES! *squeal* Thank you, thank you, thank you.

Susie Hall. My eternal optimist and beacon of light, shining on all things super-smart and super-funny, one trillion thank yous would not come close to my gratitude for all you have done for me. Thank you for always believing!

My "teach," **Arun Deva.** Thank you for all your teachings over the years and for honoring my (sometimes very silly) approach to our Ayurveda we both hold so dear. It's just the beginning, don't you think?

To the editors

Jenifer Dorsey. Thank you for keeping me streamlined while honoring my unique flair, with fewer exclamation marks. Amazing!!!!! (Oops, too many?)

Steven Tadeusik. Thank you for holding my hand to make sure this book is representative of my message *and* my spirit. *spin, spin!*

Auntie Jan. I am so honored to have had your whole-hearted commitment as part of the most special project in my life, ever!

To my loves

Tres and Alella. You two light up my LIFE! May there always be indoor snowball fights, disco balls, snuggles, lots of laughter and endless love. Let's keep living our life better and better. You are my favorite things and I love you both with all my soul.

Mom and Don. Thank you for always helping me reach my highest graces while reminding me to keep my vision within the headlights. For the many times I've started to lose faith, thanks for reminding me I've had it all along. Go Pack!

Go-Mom. Love you, Grandma! Thank you for teaching me how to be spicy and funny, while getting stuff done and appreciating the simple things. *blowing kisses*

special thanks to these loyal readers over the years

Katie C., Shelly F.,
Steven E., Karen P.,
Danielle R., Kibby M.,
Kim B., Rachel L.,
Becca C., Joy B.,
Robin M., Carolina N.,
Shoshanna B., Lisa M.,
Liz T., Kimberly M.,
Alexis M., Kristy M.,
Karina S., Neha W.,
Mary L., Diana B.,

Ya'll helped lift **heymonicab.com** off the ground and I am so grateful to be on this journey with you. Love love!

In Your Elements: A Blooming Ayurvedic Guide to Creating Your Best Life

Ordering information:

Special discounts are available on quantity purchases by corporations,
associations, bookstores, wholesalers and others. For details, please email us
at wholesale@heymonicab.com.

Published 2015 by Monica Bloom

ISBN 978-1-578-17015-2
ISBN 978-1-578-17016-9

Illustrations, book design and cover design by Monica Bloom

heymonicab.com

Printed in the United States of America

Foreword

Ayurveda. This single word captures the essence, depth and breadth of life, health and happiness. It is a science that takes a lifetime to study, and a practice that gives us the chance to live life to its fullest. It is a philosophy, an art and a way of life with roots so deep in nature that even time has not altered its foundations for the past 5,000 years.

While living and practicing Ayurveda in India for almost eight years, I became a licensed vaidya (Ayurvedic physician) which taught me that although the roots and foundations of Ayurveda are timeless, its practical usage is not. Throughout history, Ayurveda has faced many challenges — it has been repressed, revived and renewed. And the time has come for it to be revived and renewed once more, in our current world.

Monica Bloom stands to be one of the driving forces behind expanding Ayurveda's revival in the modern world. In this book, she has effectively and authentically blended the ancient and time-tested practices of Ayurveda into a simple, common-sense approach to health. Monica focuses on maintaining health and that is where we can all learn to adopt simple yet effective lifestyle habits to live a happier, healthier life.

I was one of the fortunate few first readers of *In Your Elements* and remember asking myself several times, "How did she make this so clear and simple?" It's not an easy job at all, and is one of the main reasons why there is so little authentic literature available in English for Ayurveda. With a strong, growing demand for Ayurveda happening world-wide, we need to remember to carefully select a reputable source for accurate information, and I believe this book is exactly that.

I personally want to thank Monica for investing so much time, effort, energy and love into this work, and for inviting me to be part of the process. It has been an honor to see this book first hand and be able to support its intentions of helping people live healthier with authentic and traditional knowledge of classical Ayurveda. Finally, I wish each reader a satisfying journey into Ayurveda, your Self and a lifetime of health and happiness.

With gratitude,

Dr. Jessica Vellela, BAMS
Vaidya, Founder and Chief Architect, **myayu.com**

Table of contents

Introduction

In spring 2014, I was driving into San Francisco to give an "intro to Ayurvedic basics" talk at a local fitness studio. As I came out of the tunnel on the Bay Bridge I was greeted by the majesty of the bridge towers and cityscape — a view that never gets old. I took a big inhale. This was my place. The pink shiny city stood before me as the sunrise reflected off buildings and windows almost as if it was welcoming me with open arms. Here I was, about to talk about my favorite thing in my favorite place and feeling totally in my groove, I was overcome with gratitude. With the sunroof open, I actually yelled, "EEEEE! YEESSSSSS!" and the phrase that filled my mind was, "I am SO in my element right now." Ta-dah! The name of my little Ayurvedic book was born.

Flashback to 2007. I was 31, living in San Francisco, and in the midst of "Project Monica," my biggest personal evolution when I enlisted a small army to help me unravel some emotional garbage I had been carrying around. I was done with my negativity, dramatic reactions, and so much internal sludge that was no longer serving me and it was time to let it go. In my army I enlisted a therapist, a life coach, an acupuncturist, a nutritionist, an energy intuitive — bring it on. I had no idea what I was doing but was entirely open and ready for change.

One random Sunday I was bored, pretty sad and fishing around online for… something. I didn't know what, I just wanted to run away from it all. A yoga retreat to India sounded good. That should do. India was exotic enough but a guided retreat wouldn't be totally crazy. Maybe it would offer an entry way for me to finally find peace in my heart and mind. I Googled "yoga retreat in India" and found one that had 'Ayurvedic treatments' and 'Ayurvedic food.' What I saw before my eyes was everything I had always believed about life, health, individuality and spirit, but never knew existed. A rush of energy from my chest burst to my face, my heart flew open and I instantly started sobbing as my head fell into my hands and I curled over my keyboard. After that, I paced. And paced. And thought. And cried some more. And paced. DUDE! This Ayurveda stuff was me! All me! And I knew it. To the core of my soul I knew it and I had to learn more.

No time to waste, the next day I turned down a fancy full-time graphic design job I had been interviewing for, made some phone calls, and four days later I was enrolled in an 18-month Ayurvedic program. Whee!

My first lesson in Ayurveda was, "Ayurveda shows up when you are truly ready for it." (Maybe that's what has brought you here?) I was definitely ready for it. Based on what I learned in school, I started using Ayurvedic principles and therapies to advance Project Monica until I was no longer such a big project! I learned how to exercise, eat, express myself, breathe, sleep and unravel past emotions all according to my own beautiful individuality. Ayurveda was a canopy over all these segments in life and I got to the point where I no longer needed an army. I had it all in me. Another big lesson was, "Everything starts from the inside out, not the other way around." Ayurveda gave me knowledge but most of all it gave me permission to honor my unique mind, body and spirit. I was hooked for life!

In 2008 during my studies, I was shocked that there was such limited information online — why wasn't anybody talking about this stuff? What about all the people, like me, who craved this information but didn't know it existed? Gah! Holy cow, if I could share what I learned, I could change lives and really help people heal and live better. And, according to their uniqueness! That's a big deal! I was on a mission. In 2008, I started **heymonicab.com** as an Ayurvedic resource. It was there I began teaching the foundation in simple ways specifically for living in our modern world. Where I found the entry way into my heart was to create an entry way for others.

> **Ayurveda gave me knowledge but most of all it gave me permission to honor my unique mind, body and spirit. I was hooked for life!**

In Your Elements is an extension of **heymonicab.com** and is my gift to the world. I wrote, designed and illustrated it with as much love as I could muster. If I could put a big silky bow on each copy, I would. I love it. I hope you do, too. Go learn some things about Ayurveda and more importantly, go learn a whole heck of a lot about YOU. You deserve it.

Flip through the pages and let the transformation begin

I welcome you to have an open heart and open mind. Leave your self-judgements at the door and let this be a joyful journey. Take your time. Let pieces sink in. Skip parts that don't resonate. Work it again and again. Tear out pages. Cry with it. Laugh with it. Let your heart sing through it. Get goosebumps. Even if you are going through some rough patches in your life, may this book provide light and guidance, remembering you are loved for who you are, rough patches and all. I mean, who doesn't go through rough patches (and frankly, wouldn't life be boring without them)? You will find that when you really need it, there is an abundance of help, compassion, and love from the most unexpected places. May this book be an unexpected place of loving acknowledgment and honor for who you are, the great things you do, and an opportunity to get stronger where you might be weak.

We know when we feel in sync with our bodies and minds but the hard part sometimes is to figure out what made us balanced or imbalanced. We know when we feel off but we don't always know why. That's an important missing piece! By the end of this book you'll know the whys. You'll know where you are, how to fix any issues and what you are prone to so you can prevent sickness (or imbalance) in the first place. What you will learn is ever-lasting because when you get imbalanced again in the future, you'll know what caused it and how to fix it! Hooray!

Life ebbs and flows — it will forever change so the goal is to stay balanced through all these ups, downs, and hairpin turns of life. You can always refer back to this book with other things you want to work on and start again. Even if you are feeling good and balanced for now, something might happen to throw you off kilter mentally, physically or emotionally. In fact, you can count on it. When you start to notice subtle changes, make adjustments to put your back on course.

Note: This book has Sanskrit words sprinkled throughout that look something like this: Sanskrit (SANS-krit). Some words will show up frequently and you'll begin to know them as you read about them — it will become second nature. Others, you don't need to worry about for now. Okey doke?

There are many ways to read this book and engage in the process. It should be both enlightening and fun! Here are a few ideas:

PERSONAL JOURNEY

Keep to yourself. It's all about you, just for you.

GET A GROUP TOGETHER

Go through the exercises with yoga friends, fitness buddies, work buddies, girl's wine night out (I know you) or with family.

SHARE WITH OTHERS

Share your journey, progress and discoveries on social media so others can cheerlead your progress.

MAKE IT VISIBLE

Create a vision board or keep notes handy in front of your eyes. If you see it, you WILL make it happen.

JOURNAL WITH IT

Write out your progress and how you feel. It might be fun to look back and see the progress you've made. Check in weekly, or monthly, to see how far you've come.

TEAR PAGES OUT

If some pages strike your fancy, hang them on your computer, at work or on your night stand.

INSPIRATION AND MOTIVATION

Inspire and motivate yourself and others with your new found knowledge.

THE BEST PROJECT YOU'LL EVER HAVE TO WORK ON IS YOU

What to expect from your journey ahead

A CHANGED YOU

Did you know our cells regenerate every day? They do! Every day our cells are recreated based on our thoughts, actions and foods we eat. If the quality of those thoughts, actions and foods are low, the cells will also be recreated in low quality and we might feel less than awesome. However, once we start improving our habits, the quality of our cells improve and they begin forming in new patterns. A simple example is, when we drink the right amount of water, our skin looks clean, dewey and fresh. It's because those cells now have enough water element in them and it shows on the outside. The cells changed! Now, imagine doing that with diet, exercise, breathing, meditation and stress management. You really CAN change your entire YOU.

CLARITY AND A PLAN

You will learn the uncomplicated basics of Ayurveda which include discovering your unique balance, adopting the daily routine, how to reduce toxins, a customized nutrition plan and more. You will emerge empowered to address imbalances in all areas of your life and gain clarity on what steps you can take to make it more balanced and suited to your needs.

SMALL CHANGES MAKING A HUGE IMPACT

To ensure success, keep your initial changes bite-sized. Like little delectable pieces for you to taste, savor and digest, just pick a couple things to work on while letting it sink in. Too many changes at once will set you up to fail. Not only that, but you won't know which changes had the most impact. Slow and steady is the way to go with Ayurveda. As the Ayurvedic saying goes, "Slowly we make the changes."

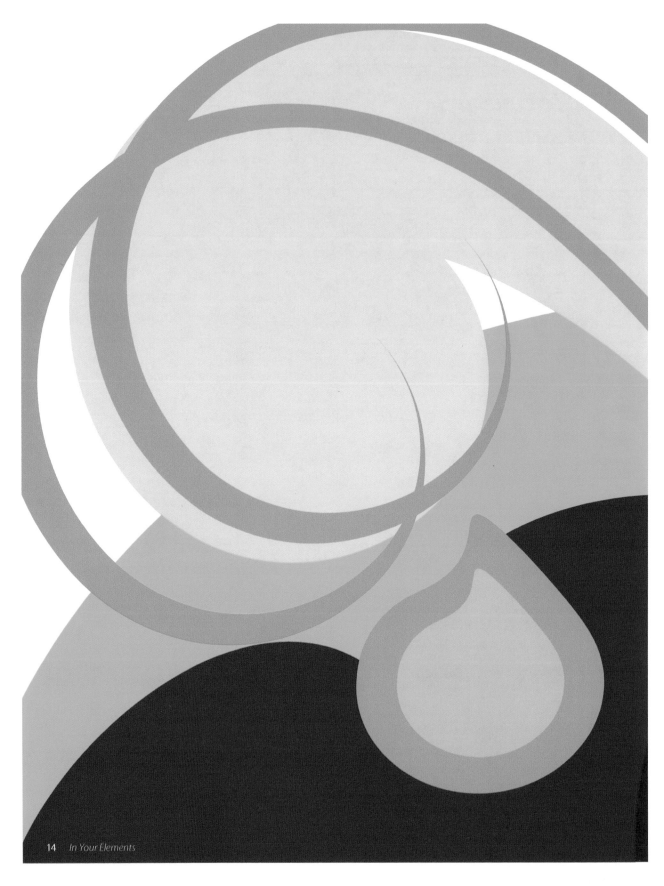

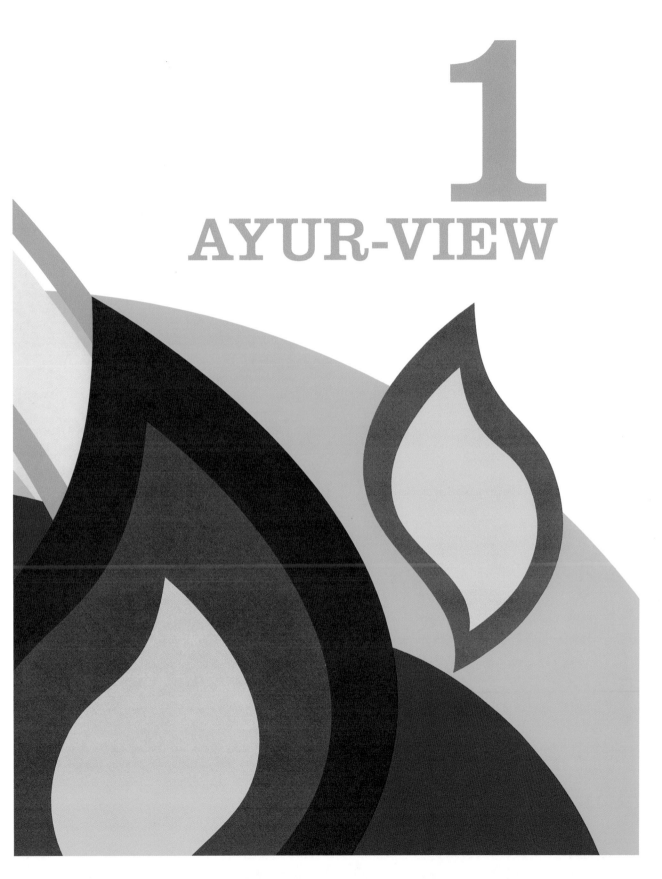

1
AYUR-VIEW

Through the eyes of Ayurveda

learn

Yoga is a sister science to Ayurveda. They have similar principles but Ayurveda is the healthcare, medicine and absolute lifestyle around yoga practice.

you matter

It's all about you, Baby! No other healing science sees you, only you, just you, as the unique burst of awesome you are.

All healing starts with the self, first. Then it can radiate outward to your friends and family.

You are the most important person you know. If you are not healthy first, nobody else will be able to benefit from your core awesomeness. Healing comes from the inside out! From there, you will begin to see the world from others' eyes while growing your compassion for others and honoring their unique selves.

AYUR-WHAT? THE PERCEPTION

Ayurveda *(EYE-yer-VAY-duh)* is a sister science to yoga and is a way to manage our health on all aspects of life as a whole.

Have you ever Googled "Ayurveda" and looked at the images? If you haven't, you should try it. You'll get one of two things: 1) a lady lying topless on a massage table with glowing brown skin, eyes closed with a slight smile. She might have schmeary goo on her skin with a poultice bag perched on top of her back. You might also see the ever famous Ayurvedic-oil-drizzle on her forehead or, 2) leaves, stems, spices and a mortar and pestle. On the surface, it looks like Ayurveda has something to do with spa treatments while using spices or herbs, somehow.

Well, that's only a tiny sliver of what Ayurveda actually is. The oil-drizzle, called shirodhara (don't worry about pronouncing that), and the poultice bags are wonderful Ayurvedic therapies. While the therapies do feel luxurious and centering, most of Ayurveda focuses on diet and lifestyle management in everyday life. Ayurveda is not meant to be expensive or elitist. Rather, it is to be shared with and used by the masses, just as it was passed down in Indian families and villages 5,000 years ago (and to this day). Contrary to the ubiquitous imagery, the most effective Ayruveda is logical, cheap, accessible and easy for anyone to incorporate. This is the version of Ayurveda that we are going to talk about and it will change your life!

> **Most of Ayurveda is diet and lifestyle management which is used on a daily basis. Accustomization and habitual use is what makes it work.**

WHAT IT REALLY IS

My friends, Ayurveda is LIFE! Big ol' life as we are today and in fact the word Ayurveda literally translates to "knowledge of life." Ayurveda embodies a whole-istic approach where mind, body and spirit work in harmony to achieve optimal health. It's kind of like the mind, body and spirit form a pyramid — if one is off kilter it will affect the others.

Ayurveda's main focus is prevention. Before we end up with a sickness or a disease, we are given clues that the body is not functioning as it should. We might notice subtle physical, mental or emotional changes — Ayurveda pays attention to those! Those signals might as well be arms waving around saying, "Hey hey! We're experiencing a slight problem in this area!" If we don't pay attention, we get sicker.

IF YOU SEEK
SOMETHING DIFFERENT
EXPECT
SOMETHING DIFFERENT

Disease doesn't come out of nowhere, it takes time to build. We can still get sick when practicing Ayurveda but a) we will get sick much less often b) the sickness won't last as long and c) you will know enough to uncover the root cause so it doesn't happen again.

Ayurveda goes broad and deep. There are eight branches under the vast umbrella of Ayurveda which include 1) internal medicine, 2) surgery, 3) pediatrics, 4) ear, nose, throat, eye diseases, 5) toxicology, 6) psychiatry, 7) rejuvenation, and 8) aphrodisiacs. Ayurveda is not a light version of healthcare, rather it is a very complex science requiring years (decades!) of training to achieve mastery. Just as there are MDs, there are also doctors of Ayurveda called vaidyas *(VAYd-yah)*. They go to medical school for five and a half years, plus an optional three for post grad, plus an optional three for their PhD, similar to what our traditional western docs do. We are not going to go deep into any one of these branches; I mention them to reinforce that Ayurveda ain't fluffy. It is an ancient, comprehensive study of us as whole physical and spiritual beings with many layers.

For our purposes, we will stick with the most easy to digest and easy to apply foundations of Ayurveda so that you start using it right away. The faster I can give you wings, the better!

Ayurveda plucks us out as individuals and provides a customized approach to health by recognizing we all have different needs.

One size does not fit all. We each have different thresholds for stress, hunger, sleep, exercise and so on. None of us look exactly the same so why would we behave the same or need the same things? Ayurveda plucks us out as individuals and provides a customized approach to health by recognizing we all have different needs. If you think this is refreshing so far, we're just gettin' started! Countless people have written to me saying how discovering Ayurveda has brought them to tears (when our heart opens, we can't help but cry) because finally there is a system that sees and honors their individuality.

HOW DOES AYURVEDA HEAL?

Based on the widespread adoption of yoga and its whole-istic philosophy, Ayurveda is already welcomed by so many of us who no longer believe in "quick fix" diets, magic pills and cure-alls that just don't work. We have become accustomed to a doctor's prescription as a bandage, which helps us feel better temporarily, but ultimately masks the root cause. Without addressing and fixing the root cause, we get further into the disease and get sicker.

Ayurveda helps us create customized life-style routines and healing techniques built just for you using natural ingredients and the dependable laws of nature.

Ayurveda works to uncover the root cause and delivers healing to the patient by bringing together nutrition, yoga/exercise, meditation, breath work, and herbs while using all five senses as a vehicle to bring the body back to its balanced state. Ayurveda makes sure the mind and spirit are equally healthy, along with our body. From there, the individual can make conscious choices to change their behaviors to avoid the health problem again in the future. An Ayurvedic practitioner may perform cleansing therapies using herbs and oils to "clean out" the imbalance and then rebuild the body through rejuvenation and revitalization therapies.

The most empowering thing about Ayurveda is that the majority of all disease can be fixed by lifestyle and dietary changes alone. Yes! That means health is totally in our hands. As we all strive to live better, feel better, look better, sleep better, weigh better, by now I think we understand there isn't an instant or magic solution. Real health takes conscious effort and adjustments as a life long practice.

WEST VS. EAST

The philosophies behind Ayurveda and modern (or, western) medicine are very different and even opposites. Ayurveda and modern medicine do not overlap much so it is important to keep them in separate buckets. However, I prefer to view them as complements rather than competitors because both have their place. I mean, what if we used both sciences where they excel? That just might be…life-transforming.

Human Being. Modern medicine sees our physical body and all its functions. The human being is made of two eyes, a nose, a heart, a brain, some blood, some cartilage, and you know the rest. Therefore, bodies must all be the same and treated the same. Modern medicine does not talk about the mind or spirit. It will address the the brain, but not the mind — two very different things as you will find out in chapter 11.

Treating the mind, body and spirit as a whole is key to Ayurvedic healing. In the physical body, Ayurveda says that while we have all the same parts, the parts are not the same size or shape in any any of us. How many people do you know with identical bodies? None, right? We are unique like snowflakes! Our eyes are different shapes and colors, our noses are different, too. Based on those subtleties, we are not the same at all. In addition to our physical

ayur-tip

The key to making lasting improvements to our health and life is to stay consistent!

ayurvedic healing techniques include

diet
daily routine
spices and herbs
skincare
breath work
stress management
meditation
exercise/yoga
pressure points
massage therapies
cleansing therapies
aromatherapy
crystals and gems therapy

body, Ayurveda highlights that we all have different capacities for stress, emotions, food, exercise, and so on — we are each completely unique.

The Focus. Modern medicine treats the symptoms so that we feel better as soon as possible. They will treat the disease and/or manage the symptoms.

True healthcare is daily, consistent, individual and intentional.

Ayurveda advocates disease prevention or "health care" as a lifelong practice. Health is not something we run to like a finish line and high five when it's over. Not even close. True healthcare (emphasis on "care") is daily, consistent, individual and intentional.

The Diagnosis. Modern medicine uses lots of tests. They test our vitals, swipe a swab or take a blood test. Once they get the test results, they will give a diagnosis on what our problem is. If it's not significant enough, they likely will send us home and tell us to come back if it gets worse.

Ayurvedic consultations in the U.S. are lengthy (like 1–2 hours) as the practitioner asks detailed questions about our health concerns and life habits. Before making a diagnosis, the practitioner takes time to observe and talk to the client by using their five senses. The goal in an Ayurvedic consultation is to uncover a) who the patient is as an individual b) the imbalance and c) the root cause.

The Treatments. Modern medicine uses a single approach by either removing the part that doesn't function well or by giving a prescription drug. We may, or may not, have to take another drug to combat the side-effects of the first drug.

Ayurvedic treatments are a multiple approach, covering many facets of our life. A revised diet, breathing techniques, exercise recommendations, herbal therapy, aromatherapy, and meditation could be prescribed. Ayurveda will treat the symptoms too, but at the same time will seek to fix the root problem. The patient will need to create real changes in their diet/lifestyle to prevent the problem from coming back.

Therapies in Ayurveda are natural — made from plants, spices, flowers, fruits, animal parts, minerals and metals — and therefore easily accepted and digested by our body. As a bonus, plant-based treatments improve the quality of our cells and tissues as we heal. That said, nature is a powerful influencer so there are contraindications for any herbal remedy. Just because Ayurveda uses natural ingredients, doesn't mean we can experiment willy nilly.

West & East

MODERN MEDICINE		AYURVEDA
	HUMAN BEING	Mind, Body, Spirit full of energy, energy controls the structure
Physical Body		
All built the same		Unique individuals
Treating the disease "disease" care	**FOCUS**	Preventing the disease "health" care
Test results	**DIAGNOSIS**	Subjective understand the patient
Stop the symptoms "quick fix" the problem	**TREATMENT**	Stop symptons and the root causes
Single approach medicine or surgery		Multiple approach diet, lifestyle, herbs, meditation, pranayama, physical treatments
Synthetic drugs		Natural therapies
n/a		Customized therapies per person
No connection to nature	**CONNECTION TO NATURE**	We are part of nature and nature governs us

Connecting to Nature. Modern medicine does not recognize our connection to nature. But modern medicine is crucial for emergencies — anything that could be life-threatening. Modern medicine can save your life.

Ayurveda emphasizes that nature is part of us, and we are part of it. We are governed by it, therefore Ayurveda uses all natural remedies (including our food) to help re-balance our health.

As we work on managing our life through Ayurveda, there is a place for both sciences to coexist. The recommendation is to practice Ayurveda daily as a lifestyle and to prevent imbalance. If we get imbalanced, we can see a western doc for help while continuing to use Ayurvedic principals to stay balanced. If we use Ayurveda correctly, our trips to the doctor may be slim to none.

Want to see my ideal world? Take a walk with me... Visualize a place where people use Ayurveda at home as a daily practice for themselves, for their children, neighbors and grandparents. They do daily pranayama (*PRAH-nuh-YAHM-uh*, regulating our breath) in the morning to keep cobwebbs from collecting in their mind and body's nooks 'n' crannies. They drink the right amount of water throughout the day. They poop at least once a day. Without fail, they do 30 minutes of exercise or yoga daily (and they love it!). They happily eat whole foods that come from nature like fruits, vegetables, healthy grains and a little meat if they need it. They look forward to going to work and they experience minimal stress because each day they make progress toward their end goal — work is one big enjoyable project or they are simply content in be-ing. They get the right amount of sleep each night and are well-rested. They only need to see a doctor for routine check ups or if something unexpected happens.

Now, let's say while doing all the right things, they get a cold. Rats! They are able to take a full day off work to rest because they understand that taking pause is the best way to heal. They make a homemade spicy tea and spend the entire day resting. They make sure to aid their digestion by eating easy-to-digest foods which helps fight the cold faster. Because of their quick self care, their cold may only last two to three days and they might only get sick once a year.

Now let's say one of them takes a joy ride on a bicycle and they fall off and sprain their wrist. Major bummer! Time for a doctor! A doctor does x-rays to confirm that it is not a break, wraps up the sprain and gives some pain medication.

In the eyes of Ayurveda, this is true healthcare. We manage most of the healthcare ourselves and leave the emergencies or chronic conditions to a doctor's expertise. As it is, our MDs are overloaded with patient appointments, only able to spend a short while with each of them. We don't go see a doctor until we are extra sick, which means they have to come up with a quick solution and move to the next patient.

As you can see the two sciences are quite different. However, within their differences is where each science excels. Ayurveda believes true healthcare starts with us, at home, with the lifestyle we choose and the foods we eat. So dance along with me to the next chapter where we will learn the ground rules of an Ayurvedic lifestyle.

2

GROUND-RULES

Get grounded

You are probably rarin' to go so let's get into the ground rules to ensure you have a solid foundation. Only when your roots are planted can you sprout, bloom and expand! The Ayurvedic ground rules are:

MACROCOSM AND MICROCOSM

IT DEPENDS

ONE SIZE DOES NOT FIT ALL

LIKE INCREASES LIKE

DO NOT RESIST YOUR URGES

SLOWLY WE MAKE THE CHANGES

YOU ARE WHAT YOU DIGEST

HEAL THROUGH THE FIVE SENSES

MIND, BODY, SPIRIT ARE TOGETHER

FOOD IS MY MEDICINE

WE ARE NATURE — MACROCOSM AND MICROCOSM

Here's something you might not have thought of: Humans, the universe, and everything in between are made of only five things. Yep, just five. Those five things are the great elements: space, air, fire, water and earth. Ayurvedic philosophy says everything found in outer space, on Earth, all the way down to our teeniest weeniest cells is made of just those five things!

A few examples include:
- outer space or holes in things (space) • wind (air) • fires (fire)
- rain, oceans and lakes (water) • the mountains and ground (earth)

Now think about your body. You have:
- holey parts (space) • parts that move other parts (air) • warm parts (fire)
- liquid parts (water) • hard parts (earth)

It might be a little hard to imagine that everything is made of just five elements, but it is similar to understanding that all paint colors can be created from red, blue and yellow. If you started mixing the elements on a palette, you would get an endless variety of everything you see. A tree, for example, is a mixture of elements. A tree has earth element in the dense trunk but there is also some space between the bark on its bumpy texture. The leaves have water in them to keep them soft as the veins move air and water through the leaf. Trees absorb sunlight, so they have a little fire in them as well. Pretty nifty, right? A tree has: space, air, fire, water and earth.

In Ayurveda, all of nature is made from and governed by the five great elements: space, air, fire, water and earth.

Spending time in nature is a perscription to heal in Ayurveda. While we are all unique, one thing stays true for all of us: we feel best when we spend time in nature because we ARE nature.

nature

Ever notice that roots and branches look just like each other? It's the same structure on each end. The roots need to be firmly planted in order to grow the top.

LIFE CHECK NATURE

Name some things that are close to nature.

_____

_____

_____

Name some things that are far from nature, or unnatural.

_____

_____

_____

Do you spend at least 30 minutes a day in nature?

_____

_____

If not, how can you fit in more time in nature?

_____

_____

_____

_____

_____

_____

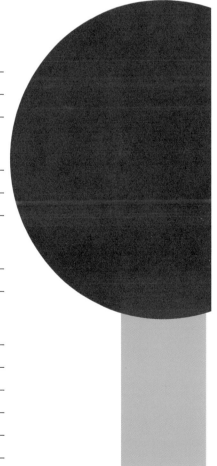

IT DEPENDS.

ONE SIZE
DOES NOT FIT
ALL.

IT DEPENDS

Because Ayurveda's focus is on the individual, we use this phrase all the time "it depends!" The solution to your health concerns depend on: your unique balance of the elements; your age; the problem; how long you've had the problem; what season it is; your diet; your exercise regimen; your emotional stabilty; your stress levels; and so on. Ayurvedic practitioners will take time to understand their patient. That is why when posed with a health question, Ayurvedic practitioners first response is, "It depends." Ayurveda does not treat disease, it treats the person.

ONE SIZE DOES NOT FIT ALL

Do you remember that store Au Coton from the '80s? They sold only cotton clothes and the entire store was "one size fits all." Um. No they didn't! None of those clothes fit me. I looked like a fluffy pleated pastel sausage in everything and it made me feel BAD because that meant that I was not part of "all" like everyone else! What a bummer. What an outsider. What a sausage.

So hear me out, while one person might feel awesome after scarfing (we do not scarf in Ayurveda, we chew very well) an entire burrito, another person might get bloated, and yet another will burp up that burrito for hours. It does not have as much to do with the burrito as much as it does with the person eating it. The first person might have a really strong digestive fire, and able to digest (metabolize if you want to be Western) it just fine. The second person might have a weaker digestive fire and the beans will make them puffy gutted. The third person might have additional heat in their body and the spicy salsa is rising (like heat does) and trying to come out. *burp* Because each one of these people are totally unique, a burrito may or may not be a good choice.

That's just one example, but there are bajillions. The same goes with exercise as people have different thresholds, abilities, flexibilities, strengths, etc. Not everyone is going to benefit from (or love) long distance running. Not everyone is going to benefit from strength training either. Even yoga, which is generally good for all people as a physical exercise and practice, offers different styles to benefit different people. Hot-bodied people should never ever ever do hot yoga! They'll get angry and pass out. Trust me.

Overall, blanket statements given to us about diet, exercise and how to stay balanced, should wave a red flag. One size does not fit all. If someone claims "this will work for everyone!" be dubious. Kleenex® will work for everyone, but that's about it. Unless you have stubble, then the Kleenex will get stuck to the stubble and — see, not even Kleenex!

truth

Authentic Ayurveda should not "sell" you anything. There are some great Ayurvedic products out there but just like anything else, be wary of any claims that "this one thing will change your entire life" because nothing is true for all people in all cases. As Ayurveda becomes more popular ('cause people love it!) be mindful of persuasive marketing so you don't do more harm than good.

LIKE INCREASES LIKE

You need to remember this: like increases like. To keep life steady on a balance beam, we use the opposite qualitites to balance us. If you are hot, eat cooling foods or jump in a pool. If you are cold, sit in a steam room or a warm bath. If you have a racing mind, use meditation or breathing to slow it down. If you are heavy, move your body and eat lighter foods. See that? By bringing in the opposite qualities, we are able to balance ourselves out in many ways.

DO NOT RESIST YOUR URGES

Hooray for urges! Our awesome bods give us the gift of urges as a signal for what it needs. So when we feel an urge, we need to honor it. Urges are different than impulses. An impulse is ego-driven and requires a quick but conscious choice, like an impulse buy of chocolate covered caramels in the check out aisle or those polka-dot sneakers that are on sale. Urges are a signal from the body that something needs to be balanced, either expelled like a sneeze, fart, pee, poop, laugh, etc., or increased like sleep or thirst.

If we hold our urges back or in, we reverse the flow which can cause stagnation, wrong flow, or clogs in our physical and/or emotional bodies. No joke, it can make us sick over time. For example, a sneeze needs to come out! Don't stifle that sneeze in your throat because you are trying to be polite in a meeting — let it out! The body wants something out of your nose and FAST, so you need to obey the bod!

The same thing applies to bathroom breaks. Despite our busy work schedules, be sure to go potty when you have to. In addition to reversing the flow or clogging channels, holding our potty actually keeps waste IN when it should be coming OUT. Don't hold it, just go. This is part of how the body functions properly by releasing what no longer serves it.

Emotions are another thing we tend to hold in. Don't stifle your emotions or they will come out in one big BLURT. Allow healthy expression of your opinions, feelings, ideas and emotions.

SLOWLY WE MAKE THE CHANGES

Ayurveda recommends adopting two to three changes for a couple weeks. Once you have these new changes incorporated like clockwork, you can add two more. And then two more. New habits need to be practiced and absorbed. And guess what — if you only make two to three changes in your diet and lifestyle over the course of six months, awesome! It's more than you were doing before.

In Ayurveda there are no drastic changes, just simple intentional, gradual progress. Think of a really dry plant. If we dump a bunch of water on it, what happens? The water runs out, down and around almost bypassing the dirt and roots! But, if we pour the water slowly, take a break, and pour a little more, the water has a chance to absorb into the soil and nurture the plant. The reason why so many people don't follow through on changes in their health is because they try too many things at once. Too much at once just can't sink in!

Don't be in a rush. You are changing your life! It took you many years of choices and routine to get where you are — you cannot change all of them in a week. OK? When six months go by you'll turn around and say, "Holy moly, I changed all that?!" Yes you did! You will be in a healthier life with new habits — because you went slowly and step-by-step.

YOU ARE WHAT YOU DIGEST

You've heard that term "you are what you eat." But in Ayurveda, we say, "you are what you digest."

Eating food is very different from digesting it. We can eat anything we can physically stick in our mouths, but that doesn't mean we will digest it well. You see, our digestive power varies from person to person, therefore foods that will benefit one person might not benefit another. One person can eat a salad and feel awesomely light and energized, while another person gets instantly bloated and grumbly-tummied. We have different levels of digestive power and if we don't digest our food well the old food stuffs turn into goopy toxins called ama *(AH-muh)*. Ama is the root cause of most disease so it is super important to eat foods that we can digest well.

HEAL THROUGH THE FIVE SENSES

The five senses are our receptors of the outside world. In fact, our body is so good at using all of these senses that when one sense is lost, the others increase as the body's way to keep the information coming in! Because the senses are the receptors of so much information, they can get overtaxed and overloaded. When the senses get over-used, under-used, or misused, the body's receptors get crossed with conflicting waves of information. I'm sure you've heard of sensory overload and that's exactly what it means. We are given too much information to process or digest causing an overload of the senses, which can also cause toxins. What we experience with our senses is delivered to the body and those experiences will either balance or imbalance us.

The senses play the main role in how we receive and digest information, since Ayurveda uses them as vehicles to deliver various therapies and healing to the body and mind. Included are aromatherapy, sight therapy, the six tastes, touch or massage, and mantras or music therapy. Depending on what the imbalance is, we will choose the therapy that most directly affects that sense.

MIND, BODY, SPIRIT ARE NOT SEPARATE

Our squishy innards, our bones, our skin, our thoughts, our relationships, our breath, our homes, our food, our happiness, our crankiness and our unique funkiness are all part of who we are. All of those things can be balanced through Ayurveda. Our body, mind and spirit are all connected, so our life connects to our body and our body to our life — they fuel each other. They go hand-in-hand.

Mind. The mind is the driver. The body doesn't just go around doing things all by itself. If you have a glass of water in front of you, the mind tells your arm and hand to reach for it, pick it up, and then lift it to your mouth. The mind makes choices and the body follows suit. Based on those choices, everything else happens.

Body. Body is our physical self. *poke* The body is made of the five elements (space, air, fire, water and earth) and experiences life through the five senses. It is the physical formation of everything we take in including what we eat; how we exercise; what and how we think and our elements. If our body does not get what it needs our mind will be negatively affected.

Spirit. The mind and body are pretty easy to undersand, but what is spirit? Spirit is essentially the soul. The soul or spirit is the most subtle yet most important part of who we are. The soul is our higher self and we often need quiet to listen to the spirit. When our spirit is "off" path, our mind will not make the right choices and therefore our body might suffer. If our mind does make the right choices and body does the action it's instructed to do, then our spirit SOARS.

FOOD IS MY MEDICINE

Who has heard someone say, "Oh man, I better take heartburn medicine before I eat these spicy chicken wings because they always give me heartburn!" Um, let me shine a light on something: if you don't eat the wings, you won't need the medicine. Your body is telling you those wings are no bueno for you.

Food is our main source of nourishment as our body is literally made of the food we give it. It's that simple! If we feed our bodies good things, they'll feel good. If we feed them junk, they will feel (and look) like junk — the bod may start to break down in places, become inflamed or dry in others, hold on to extra fat and so on. As these things happen, we will likely look to some kind of medicine to help us feel better.

Pssst…Guys, food is the medicine! Instead of taking medicine, let's change the foods we are eating. Let's make a different choice and pick out foods that benefit our individual awesomeness. We will get deep into "new-trition" in chapter 7 so hang tight. You will soon know exactly which foods are best for you.

Now that your brain is full of good information on the ground rules, it's time to talk about you. Much of Ayurveda is not general at all, but specific and ever-changing depending on you, your life and how nature changes around you. So let's hold hands and step into the next (and most exciting) part of your journey as we learn about doshas.

nourish

Eating foods we can digest well is one of the most crucial ways we can maintain our health.

philosophy

Do not mistake the terms diet and diet.

What we feed our body to nourish it with a good regimen is a good diet.

To be ON a diet is completely different. If any foods you eat are claiming to be "diet" foods or "low fat," skip them. Any foods that provide nourishment are perfect as they are from nature and should not be altered.

In Your Elements

3

YOU-NIQUE

What's a dosha?

learn

The word "dosha" literally means imperfection.

There is a difference between space and air. Space is what might seem "empty" or a hole. Air creates movement like the wind or vibrations going through a musical instrument.

I think you're gonna love this! Everyone's favorite part of Ayurveda are the doshas *(DOE-shuz)*. From the five elements (space, air, fire, water, earth), come three energies. Those three energies are called doshas. The doshas are vata, the energy of movement; pitta, the energy of transformation; and kapha, the energy of lubrication and structure.

Our bodies are comprised of all three doshas and each dosha is made of different elements. Together the doshas combine to form our physical body. Each dosha has specific functions, qualities, and effects. The time of day, the seasons, and our life cyles are all governed by doshas. Doshas create balance in the body and when out of balance, the doshas create the defect, or the disease. We have all three doshas in each of us but we have them in unique combinations. This unique combination is what creates YOU and is the reason why Ayurveda is highly individualized. Yep. The doshas are the crowd pleaser part of Ayurveda where everyone says, "Yay! Who am I?"

We will get to that right quick, but before you take the dosha test (p. 53) to find out which dosha(s) you are, let's meet the doshas one by one. It is important to become familiar with their energy, physicality, qualities and actions. There will be one or two doshas that best describe you, quickly followed by a sparkle in your soul that says, "Hey, that's me!" You might also recognize your family members and friends. Doshas are definitely the most fun to learn, so without further delay, let's meet these three doshas…

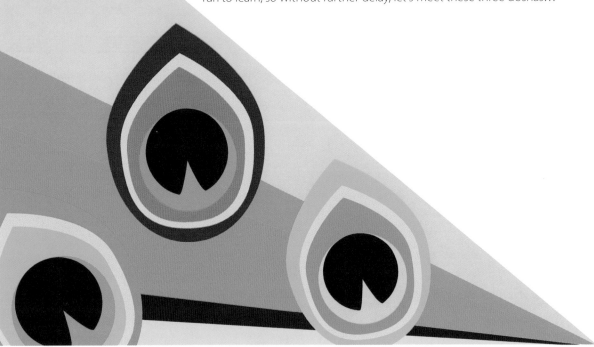

Introducing, the doshas!

VATA DOSHA IS MADE OF SPACE + AIR

Vata is the energy of movement and is made of the elements space and air. In nature, vata energy is the wind — it is subtle, fast, cold and moves quickly.

PITTA DOSHA IS MADE OF FIRE + WATER

Pitta is the energy of transformation and is made of the elements fire and water. In nature, pitta energy is the sun, it is masculine, hot and fiery and transforms anything in its path.

KAPHA DOSHA IS MADE OF WATER + EARTH

Kapha is the energy of lubrication and structure and is made of water and earth. In nature, kapha energy is the moon, it is feminine, cool and moist and is responsible for all creation.

VATA
THE ENERGY
OF MOVEMENT

Temperment: creative and energetic
Elements: air + space
Qualities: cold, dry, light, mobile, subtle, rough
Season: fall through mid-winter
Nature: wind
Main location: colon

Vata dosha is responsible for our every move including subtle movements like the heart beating, blood circulating, and eyes blinking to very gross movements like dancing, running and playing air guitar. Vata governs our colon, ears, heart beats and breath. In fact, vata is referred to as "king of the doshas" because pitta and kapha cannot move without it. Vata plays a large role because it is involved in almost every function of the body.

Windy types that they are, vatas talk fast, walk fast, create fast and worry fast. Vata people are thin with a small frame and lack of insulation (fat). They have a slender physique, an oval-shaped face and their hair is thin, dry, and frizzy. They are delicate in physical build and emotional stability. Their moods and mind changes easily. Vatas are a bit bird-like, flitting from one thing to the next, sometimes out of pure spontenaeity and other times soaring with intention and grace. Since vata people are made of air and space, they don't have a lot holding them together so they will go quickly out of balance and quickly come back into balance.

Vata Personality. Balanced vatas are creative, spiritual, eager, quick thinkers and quick adapters. They are exhuberant and their positive energy attracts others. Vatas in all their glory are effervescent, contagiously energetic and delightfully invigorating — the people you might say "light up the room." Vatas are happiest when they are warm and have a calm, peaceful mind, which allows their creativity to soar.

dosha fun

The vata mind lives in the future. They love to "what-if" the future with stories of 1,000 possible scenarios. Vatas need to remember to stay present. Most of what they put their energies and worries into hasn't even happened yet.

If vata doesn't stick to a reliable schedule and eat grounding foods, they can fly away like a kite without a string.

Vatas learn quickly and forget just as fast.

, slender, bones
visible around
joints

- Oval face, small eyes
  and lashes, long nose,
  long fingers

- Skin is dry and cool, nails
  are brittle

- Skin color is olive or light
  brown — tans easily

- Dry, curly or frizzy hair

- They talk a lot and use
  their hands for emphasis

- Chronic multi-taskers

- Talk fast, walk fast, think
  fast, easily fatigued

- Always late

- Spontaneous, eager
  and "trust their gut"

- They are artists, designers,
  teachers, actors, dancers

• • • • • • • •

Vatas are vibrant pollinators as they provide a creative jump-start, but often need help from others to plan and produce the rest because they will quickly move on to the next thing. Vatas are not detail-oriented and despite best intentions, are chronically late. They always change their mind — if they had someone to lay out their outfits maybe they could leave on time. "Ballet flats with these leggings? No. This shirt with these jeans? Hmm. But then I need a necklace…which one…?"

They do best with projects ecompassing many facets so they can stay creative in each part. They love expansive space to breathe, move and wiggle. If a vata person is in an environment that is dark, stagnant and cluttered, they will get depressed very quickly. The do not tolerate criticism well because they have delicate confidence and their feelings get hurt easily. They are delicate and deeply affected by sad things, so they have to be careful what they watch on TV. They are dramatic beings, swinging like a pendulum in a life-long quest to stay in the middle ground. When they are "on" they are SO on, but when they are "off" they are SO off. The good news is, they quickly forget what they were "off" about and can quickly resume singing happy as a bird.

Vata out of balance. Vatas are prone to imbalances like: anxiety, worry, panic, mood swings, chronic fatigue, memory loss, constipation, dry skin, pain, spasms, depression and osteoperosis. Because they are the energy of movement, their minds and bodies are constantly going, like fidgeting or wiggling their legs when they sit. This constant motion is a result of a vata increase and can also create a vata increase. When vatas get cold, they lose their mind! Their concentration flies out the window as they become moody or confused, forgetful or inattentive, which can make them highly inefficient.

Overall when vatas have too much motion it turns them into a tornado of confusion, self-doubt and feelings like they have lost control. Vatas are the people who will say, "I need my space." Their minds tend to race to the future creating imaginary outcomes.

Vata needs. Nutritionally, vatas can add structure, grounding and warmth by eating warm "comfort" foods with healthy oils, including ghee. Easy and balancing dishes for vata are non-vegetarian soups, stews and one pot meals. Vata appetite is erratic, meaning, sometimes they will eat like a bird and other times they will be an endless pit. Vatas lack fire and water elements which makes them prone to constipation because of their cold and dry qualities. Oils and sauces lubricate the body to counterbalance the rough and dry qualities while warm foods help balance the cold qualities. This will help our vata friends maintain regular digestion.

Vatas need a reliable schedule that provides some structure and reliability, otherwise they will be too worried to be happy or productive. Vatas think pittas are hilarious and admire their organization. Vatas love kapha hugs and are grounded by kapha's steady, peaceful nature.

VATAS GET IMBALANCED BY:
OVER-STIMULATION, COLD/DRY ENVIRONMENT, COLD/DRY FOODS, MULTI-TASKING, MOVING TOO MUCH AND/OR TOO FAST.

VATAS NEED:
STRUCTURE, GROUNDING, WARMTH, HEAVINESS AND OILINESS.

A GOOD MANTRA FOR VATAS:
"STAY PRESENT" AND "SLOW DOWN."

LIFE CHECK FRIENDS AND FAMILY

Who are the vatas in your life?

_____

_____

_____

_____

_____

_____

_____

_____

_____

_____

_____

_____

connection

The phrase "change like the wind" describes a vata perfectly. Think of vata as a dry crispy leaf flipping end-over-end in the wind.

dosha fun

Lying in total relaxation (savasana) after yoga class is challenging for vatas at first because it is in their nature to move, but the grounded stillness will be exactly what they need and crave.

PITTA
THE ENERGY OF
TRANSFORMATION

Temperment: leadership and intellect
Elements: fire + water
Qualities: hot, sharp, slightly oily, mobile, smooth
Season: late spring through summer
Nature: sun
Main location: small intestines

Pitta dosha is responsible for digestion and transformation including our food, thoughts, emotions, and intelligence. Pitta governs our eyes, skin, liver, blood (anything red has pitta in it), small intestines, and digestive fire. There is a very important connection between pitta and our digestive fire or, agni (p. 92). Pitta is the only dosha with the fire element so, the state of pitta dosha affects how well our agni functions. Pitta's responsibility is to digest and assimilate nutrients, while separating the useful food from the waste — kind of like sorting the whites from the brights in the laundry.

Pitta-type people have a medium and muscular build, sensitive skin, and they usually run hot. They have sharp facial features, penetrating blue or green eyes and receding hairline or early graying (because they are constantly thinking their hot little hairs turn gray and fall out). Pittas are well-organized, move with intent, and pre-plan everything. Their analytical nature will drive them to ask a bajillion questions before making a sound decision. They are also overly concerned about time, often doing a drive-by before appointments so they know precisely how long it takes to get there. Pittas are sharp in mind and also sharp in tongue — their words can feel jarring at times.

Since pittas are high-performers and often overloaded, they don't beat around the bush as they are trying to find the quickest and best solution. Pittas are fantastic improvisors, negotiators and problem-solvers because they live in the present. Just like a slowly growing fire, pittas take a moderate amount of time to go out of balance and a moderate amount of time to come back in to balance.

learn

Visualize pitta as a hot, slick oil moving like a snake while transforming everything in its path.

Heated problems with the word 'burn' or suffix "itis" in it are usually pitta problems.

dosha fun

In an office meeting, pittas are the ones fanning their faces with paper, the ones holding or running the agendas, and the first ones to play "devil's advocate."

Sharpness in vata is like a needle — thin irritability. Sharpness in pitta is like a knife — sharp, curt.

PIttas really dislike flourescent lights and are especially sensitive to them.

Pittas can apply henna for cooling!

● ● ● ● ● ● ● ● ●

how to spot a pitta

- Athletic, muscular or medium build
- Sharp facial features (nose, chin, eyes)
- Skin is pink, fair, freckled maybe some moles
- Blue, green or "sharp" eyes
- Early graying, balding, or receding hairline
- Smooth, silky, straight hair
- Their words will feel and sound sharp
- Chronically witty
- Need glasses or contacts
- Extremely punctual
- Asks a lot of questions
- They are in sales, athletics, politics, law, leadership roles or entrepreneurs

● ● ● ● ● ● ● ● ●

Pitta personality. Balanced pittas are joyful, persuasive, have a quick-witted sense of humor, and easily attract others to follow their direction. Pittas have fiery personalities and are happiest when things go their own way — they just might debate and argue until you agree with their point of view. If they can embody lightheartedness and "chill out" accepting not everything will go their way, their natural ability to inspire and teach everyone around them will shine.

Thriving on competition with a natural ability to lead, pittas make great lawyers, athletes, politicians and business owners. Pittas are mega-organized and will get irritated if things are messy or out of place. Because pitta governs the eyes, pittas see everything down to the tiniest detail. If they see a spelling error they will have to correct it. If they see splotches in the kitchen sink they will have to clean it up. If there is a mess or disarray in their line of site, their mind will not be able to focus and when pittas are out of focus they get irritable. They will use phrases like, "See from my perspective" partly as persuasion and partly to convey the solution to others.

Pittas out of balance. Pittas are prone to heated imbalances like sunburn, heartburn, hypertension, tension headaches, increased stress, irritability and even road rage! They have a pretty high threshold, but eventually their stress levels will cause burnout. Pittas do get angry but they are not easily angried — they tend toward frustration and irritability as their go-to negative emotions, mostly if they feel others are not doing their part or are not following the rules. Because pitta is related to our digestive fire, pitta digestion can run too hot or sharp resulting in an acidic stomach, heartburn, and diarrhea.

Pitta needs. Nutritionally, pittas need grounding, cool, fresh foods like healthy grains, fruits, vegetables and proteins. Balanced pittas will crave sweet fruits, salads, legumes, breads, rice, milk and cucumber water. Pittas should be careful of excess salt, cheese, hot spices, sour fruits, yogurt and alcohol because these foods can easily cause imbalance. Because of their fire element, pittas have strong digestion, are always hungry and can eat almost anything. Warning: if a pitta is hungry and they don't get fed, watch out! Their joy will turn into a raging and fierce fire.

As their default, pittas always create a reliable schedule but they need to understand that not all things always go according to plan. Even rules get broken sometimes *gasp!*. Relaxation can be hard for a pitta but it's necessary for them to relax to keep from going into overdrive. Pittas are the least emotional of the three doshas because their nature is rooted in transformation and action.

Pittas are brilliant if you need action or problem-solving, but they are not care-takers. If you need sympathy or nurturing, talk to a kapha instead. Pittas appreciate vata's creative problem-solving and love kapha's consistent reliability.

PITTAS GET IMBALANCED BY:
TOO MUCH HEAT, COMPETITION, HIGH STRESS, THE SUN, SPICY OR SOUR FOODS.

PITTAS NEED:
GROUNDING, COOL BREEZES, SERENITY, RELAXATION, SPARE TIME.

A GOOD MANTRA FOR PITTAS:
"HAVE COMPASSION" AND "LET IT GO, SURRENDER."

LIFE CHECK FRIENDS AND FAMILY

Who are the pittas in your life?

_____

_____

_____

_____

_____

_____

_____

_____

_____

_____

_____

_____

dosha fun

Pittas are perfectionists. Getting bogged down in the details is often what causes them to be workaholics.

Pittas hold in stress and will take projects on themeselves instead of delegating (it's that control thing). So pittas, remember other people have good ideas too and they are also capable of doing a good job. Teach them how to fish so that you can keep strategizing and planning without over-taxing yourself.

In Your Elements

KAPHA
THE ENERGY
OF LUBRICATION
AND STRUCTURE

Temperment: steady and nurturing
Elements: water + earth
Qualities: cold, wet, heavy, static, dense, dull
Season: spring
Nature: moon
Main location: stomach and chest

Kapha dosha creates our physical building blocks and is responsible for keeping our tissues strong and supple. Kapha is our lubrication, mucus, reproductive fluids and is responsible for building our tissues. It is the glue that binds the body together. Kapha is creation! Kapha nurtures and supports vata and pitta — mentally, emotionally and physically.

Kaphas have a solid or voluptuous build and though they have a strong presence, they are soft-spoken and shy. Kapha-type people are very strong, jolly, sweet and highly structured in both mind and body. They have thick porcelain skin (they don't wrinkle easily!) and thick hair. Their eyes are round with thick eyelashes and they have a strong bright smile. Kaphas are the sturdiest of the three doshas capable of handling a lot of work with endless patience. Since kaphas are made of water and earth, they are heavy and slow in nature, so it takes them a very long time to get out of balance and a very long time to come back into balance.

Kapha personality. Everybody loves a kapha! Balanced kaphas are peacemakers, empathetic caretakers, joyous hosts and give the best hugs, ever. They are always happy, extremely tolerant, patient and they are the first ones to offer a helping hand. Kaphas love to cheerlead — their faces and hearts light up with pride when others succeed. Their mind is steady, their attitude is positive and their bodies are very strong. Their presence allows others to rest easy because kaphas will never judge, they always listen, and rarely get angry. Kaphas are happiest when they are in a warm, dry climate and when engaged in light activities like gardening, cooking, or knitting. They are powerful singers — healthy lubrication around the vocal chords makes them a natural.

dosha fun

Without kapha, vata and pitta would be a windy inferno. Kapha cools the heat and calms the wind, balancing the two with cooling nourishment so they don't burn everything up.

Kaphas are the healthiest of the three doshas because they have such a strong foundation. They do not ride an emotional roller-coaster like a vata, nor do they carry stress like a pitta.

If you have someone in your life/family that you call the "glue," chances are they are a kapha.

- Large frame, big bones, strong joints
- Round face, big eyes, lush lashes, button nose (face of an angel)
- Strong nails, big knuckles
- Skin is cool, moist and thick
- Skin color is even, complexion is pure
- Thick, wavy, oily hair
- Often shy, quiet and listen more than they talk
- Strong endurance
- Very patient, slow moving
- Can be lazy or a "couch potato"
- Would rather follow than lead
- Puts everyone else first
- Often work in hospitality or service jobs. Secretaries, nurses, chefs, construction workers, human resources.

········

Kaphas do not like change and feel most comfortable in their routine. They frequent the same restaurants, order the same entrée over and over, and might not move far from their hometown. Kaphas take a very long time to make a decision. A little on the lazy side, they would rather someone else make decisions so all they have to do is follow. You might hear a kapha say, "Whatever you think!" or "I'll follow your lead." Give kapha a list of projects to do and consider it done. Kaphas have strong endurance but can overextend themselves, leaving nothing left to nourish themselves. They are the ultimate people pleasers and have a hard time saying "no" because they don't like to upset others, create conflict, or stir the pot. They will often take on way too much just to keep the peace. However, if kaphas don't ask for reprieve, they might take on "poor me" syndrome and that negative weight can be felt by everyone. It is not easy to exhaust or upset a kapha, but once you've upset a them, they get downright mean and hold a grudge. The best thing kaphas can do is ask for what they need. Others will always assume they are OK because of their happy-go-lucky nature, so kaphas need to ask!

Kapha out of balance. Kaphas are prone to imbalances like weight gain, lethargy, cloudiness of mind, cystic acne, allergies, increased mucus, water retention and depression. Kaphas can get lonely if they don't have enough "people" time. Being with others invigorates kaphas — they feel lighter and inspired when in the company of vivacious vatas or strategic-thinking pittas. Because of their heavy and static nature, it is easy for kapha to collect things.

Kapha needs. Kapha appetite and metabolism is slow, so they should skip a meal to remain content and happy. Fasting is necessary for kaphas because it gives their low digestive fire a chance to catch up and process any old food stuffs hanging around. Kapha is watery, so they need to soak up the excess water with airy and dry foods (veggies, fruits, salads, legumes). A light, warm, spicy vegetarian diet is best for kapha to heat them up and keep them light on their feet.

Kaphas love to shop the sales and buy things in multiples! They are the ones to buy three pairs of the same jeans in different colors or seven of the same spatula because they were on bulk discount. One of the best things kapha can do for themselves is lighten the load from past emotions and material things.

Kaphas are the most emotional dosha and cry the most easily (all that water in them comes right out). Go to a kapha for emotional support but not for a strategic plan of action. Kaphas brighten up and gain a spring in their step when surrounded by the lively energy of a vata. Kaphas have strong admiration for pitta's strong abilities to lead the way.

KAPHAS GET IMBALANCED BY:
HEAVY EMOTIONS, EXCESS FOOD, EXCESS MATERIAL THINGS, LACK OF PHYSICAL MOVEMENT.

KAPHAS NEED:
LIGHTNESS, WARMTH, MOVEMENT, DRYNESS AND SPICE.

A GOOD MANTRA FOR KAPHAS IS:
"LET GO OF WHATEVER DOES NOT SERVE ME" AND "GET UP AND DANCE!"

LIFE CHECK FRIENDS AND FAMILY

Who are the kaphas in your life?

_____

_____

_____

_____

_____

_____

_____

_____

_____

Doshas at their best

dosha fun in the animal kingdom

The light, chripy, free-spirited, graceful, but often anxious vatas can be represented by a BIRD. They eat mostly veggies, some fruits and a little wormy protein once in a while.

The strong-willed leader, who is muscular, competitive, athletic, meat-eating and sometimes ferocious, pitta can be represented by a LION. They eat mostly meat and if not fed will attack anything in its path.

The slow-moving, gentle, retentive, vegetarian, peaceful and strong dosha is kapha, which can be represented by an ELEPHANT. Even on a veggie diet, these animals are the strongest, heaviest animals with the biggest hearts.

GO TO A VATA IF YOU NEED...

uplifting energy, a breath of fresh air, creative ideas, invigoration, inspiration, light-heartedness, a fresh approach to situations, spontenaeity, exploring future possibilities.

GO TO A PITTA IF YOU NEED...

advice without emotion, problem-solving, action planning, witty humor, organization, strategy, leadership, mentoring or staying present and focused.

GO TO A KAPHA IF YOU NEED...

emotional comfort, someone to listen, a good meal, a great hug, stamina, reliability, empathy, accessorizing, or reminiscing fond memories.

EMBRACE YOU

I get lots of questions from my readers about their own unique balance. Sometimes vatas and pittas say, "I wish I was a kapha!" Oh, come on now, kaphas have their vices too, but sometimes we do wish we could become something we are not. Maybe we wish we were more organized like pitta. Or maybe we wish we had more creativity like vata. And, of course, we all wish for more peace of mind and compassion like a kapha.

Friends, I have some news: YOU are always going to be YOU. You cannot become a different dosha if it's not in your nature. Animals don't wish they were different, they're just the best animal that they are. They thrive by focusing on their strengths and positive qualities rather than their weaknesses. While you are discovering who you are, embrace the way you are unique.

Yay! So, what's my dosha?

Now that you know more about the doshas, you might have some inklings about who you are. You might be a blend of two doshas or one might make you shout, "That's ME!" You could also probably think of people in your life who are specific doshas. Awesome, you should be stoked because this is the best part! It's time to officially find out who you are. Let's take a dosha quiz.

TAKING THE QUIZ

Answer each question twice. One is based on your prakruti *(prah-KROO-tee)* and one based on your vikruti *(vih-KROO-tee)*. On occasion, you might feel like two answers are true for you. If that happens, pick the very best answer and if it's too tough to decide, choose both answers.

PRAKRUTI IS NATURAL, PURE, AUTHENTIC, YOU.

VIKRUTI IS YOUR CURRENT IMBALANCE.

Prakruti: Choose the best answer (v, p, k) based on what your *natural tendencies* are, not necessarily who you are today or who you wish to be. This should be based on your core self. Prakruti is natural, pure, authentic, you at the healthiest time of your life.

Vikruti: Choose the best answer (v, p, k) based on who you are today. Some answers might vary from the prakruti column and some might be the same. Vikruti is your current imbalance.

Note: There is no comparison against other people. And, there are no good or bad dosha combinations. OK, go have fun!

a favorite resource

myAyu.com

My girl, Jessica Vellela, BAMS, is one of the few Westerners to become an Ayurvedic Physician (Vaidya) in India.

With her impressive knowledge, she has created **myayu.com,** a wonderful online platform using modern tools. You can sign up for various programs with Jessica and her team of health experts, depending on your needs. Tell them Monica B sent you!

I AM UNLIKE ANYONE I KNOW

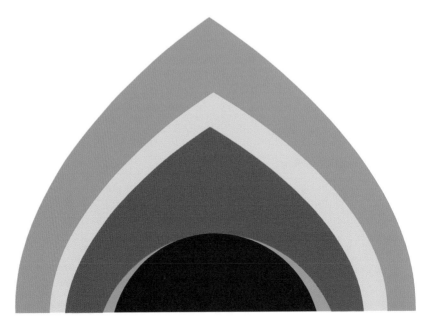

01. PHYSIQUE
v) Slender, hardly gain weight
p) Medium build with good muscle tone
k) Well built, curvy and tend to gain weight easily

PRAKRUTI: _____ VIKRUTI: _____

02. SKIN
v) Olive, dry, thin and itches often
p) Pink, flushed and/or moles and freckles
k) Porcelain, smooth and soft

PRAKRUTI: _____ VIKRUTI: _____

03. HAIR
v) Dry, thin, brittle and/or frizzy
p) Silky and straight, early graying or
   receding hairline
k) Thick, full, lustrous, wavy and slightly oily

PRAKRUTI: _____ VIKRUTI: _____

04. FACE
v) Oval and thin
p) Triangular with sharp features (pointed chin,
   prominent jaw line)
k) Round and soft features

PRAKRUTI: _____ VIKRUTI: _____

05. EYES
v) Small, they feel dry often (usually brown)
p) Medium, almond shaped, penetrating
   (usually blue or green)
k) Big, round in shape, moist, full eyelashes
   (any color)

PRAKRUTI: _____ VIKRUTI: _____

06. HANDS
v) Dry, rough, slender fingers and knuckles;
   dry, thin nails
p) Moist, pink, medium fingers and knuckles;
   pink soft nails
k) Firm; thick fingers and knuckles; strong and
   smooth nails

PRAKRUTI: _____ VIKRUTI: _____

07. JOINTS
v) Small, prominent bones and often crack
p) Medium and loose
k) Large sturdy with lots of muscle surrounding

PRAKRUTI: _____ VIKRUTI: _____

08. ACTIVITIES
v) Very active, always on the go, multi-tasking,
   constantly thinking
p) I like to think before I do anything
k) I am steady and graceful, don't like to rush

PRAKRUTI: _____ VIKRUTI: _____

09. DECISIONS
v) I take leaps of faith often without much
   information
p) I ask lots of questions and gain full clarity
   before making a decision
k) I take a long time to decide and/or prefer
   someone else make the decision

PRAKRUTI: _____ VIKRUTI: _____

10. PACE
v) I walk fast and talk fast
p) My actions are very thoughtful and precise
k) I like a slower pace, enjoy my process, and take my
   time to accomplish things

PRAKRUTI: _____ VIKRUTI: _____

11. SLEEP
v) Tend to toss and turn, I wake up early
p) Light sleeper but if I wake up, I can go back to
   sleep easily
k) Heavy sleeper

PRAKRUTI: _____ VIKRUTI: _____

12. APPETITE
v) Sometimes hungry, sometimes not, I feel anxious
   or weak if I don't eat
p) I always feel hungry, if I don't eat I get irritable
   and angry
k) I don't feel very hungry, I can easily skip meals

PRAKRUTI: _____ VIKRUTI: _____

13. POOP
v) I tend to have constipation and go a day or
   two without pooping
p) I poop more than once every day and sometimes
   poops are loose
k) I poop every day and it's usually consistent

PRAKRUTI: _____ VIKRUTI: _____

14. VOICE

v) Weak, hoarse or shreaky

p) Strong voice, sometimes loud

k) Deep, has good tone, people compliment
   my voice

PRAKRUTI: _____ VIKRUTI: _____

15. EMOTIONS

v) Born worrier, often anxious and nervous

p) If things don't happen my way, I feel irritable
   and angry

k) Always happy, but can get lonely and depressed

PRAKRUTI: _____ VIKRUTI: _____

16. FAVORITE WEATHER

v) Hot and humid

p) Cool weather

k) Warm and dry

PRAKRUTI: _____ VIKRUTI: _____

17. SWEAT

v) Never sweat, unless working very hard

p) A lot and kinda stinky

k) Sweat easily when working or if it's humid.
   Smells pleasant, like a baby.

PRAKRUTI: _____ VIKRUTI: _____

18. MEMORY

v) Learn quickly and forget quickly

p) Remember what's important

k) Slow to remember, but never forget

PRAKRUTI: _____ VIKRUTI: _____

19. RISK-TAKING

v) Love to be spontaneous

p) Won't make a decision unless there is a plan

k) Don't like risks and move cautiously until
   someone else goes first

PRAKRUTI: _____ VIKRUTI: _____

20. STAMINA

v) Activities in spurts and I get tired very easily

p) I have medium stamina

k) I can work long hours and not get tired

PRAKRUTI: _____ VIKRUTI: _____

21. MIND

v) Racing

p) Impatient

k) Calm and happy

PRAKRUTI: _____ VIKRUTI: _____

22. PERSONALITY

v) "Can I change my mind?"

p) "I want it done my way"

k) "Don't worry, be happy"

PRAKRUTI: _____ VIKRUTI: _____

23. HEALTH PROBLEMS

v) Pain, constipation/bloating, anxiety
   and depression

p) Skin infections/redness, heart burn, hypertension

k) Allergies, congestion and weight gain

PRAKRUTI: _____ VIKRUTI: _____

24. HOBBIES

v) Art, drawing, painting, dance and travel

p) Sports, politics, news radio, anything that gets my
   adrenaline pumping

k) Nature, gardening, reading and knitting

PRAKRUTI: _____ VIKRUTI: _____

Add up your V, P, and Ks from the prakruti and
vikruti columns. Tally your scores below.

PRAKRUTI: V) _____ P) _____ K) _____

VIKRUTI: V) _____ P) _____ K) _____

The highest number in the prakruti row is your
natural balance or, where you started from. The
highest number in the vikruti row is your
balance today. The difference between the two
is the dosha that has imbalanced over the
years. This pin points exactly where to focus to
bring your balance back.

Are you a vata, pitta or kapha? Or a blend of two?
We will have one or two dominant doshas. If
the numbers are close it means you have a
primary and secondary dosha. Based on your
quiz answers, it will be clear where the doshas
show up in your body and mind.

My prakruti is: _____

My vikruti is: _____

HOORAY! YOU KNOW YOUR DOSHA!

Prakruti and vikruti

OK, you just did a dosha test which highlighted where you started from naturally and where you are today. If yours match, congratulations, you have optimal health! Most likely they don't match and that's a beautiful thing too because it means there is a wonderful opportunity for you to make new choices and embody new habits to live better according to YOU!

People have asked me if our prakruti changes over a lifetime and the answer is no. Your prakruti never changes, it is always your unique make-up. Forever. However, over time, life happens. We have good habits, bad habits, we get stressed, we have emotional traumas, we adjust our life according to the season, and so on. The result of all those life happenings is vikruti or, in other words, when your doshas have gone off course. In that case, we will need to work on re-balancing vikruti (imbalanced doshas) to get back to prakruti (your natural balance). You follow?

LET'S WALK THROUGH AN EXAMPLE

Our friend Matty has a vata-pitta prakruti. Over time, Matty has accumulated a vata vikruti. Matty has an equal balance of vata and pitta doshas and only a little kapha dosha. Therefore, Matty's prakruti is vata-pitta.

Now, Matty has a new job that is highly stressful. He has started to drink more coffee and doesn't have enough time to cook warm meals so he's eating cold sandwiches and salads on the run. To help relieve job stress, he began over-exercising. Matty's mind has started to race, especially when he wakes up in the middle of the night and can't get back to sleep. Matty also starts noticing typical vata-imbalances like constipation, dry skin, and he sometimes has problems concentrating. On the surface Matty will seem more like a vata person than his natural vata-pitta self.

Because of these habits, Matty has increased the space and air elements, as well as movement, which are all related to vata dosha. Matty now has a vata imbalance and therefore vata vikruti. Matty's prakruti is still vata-pitta (never changing, remember, it's his natural combo) but his vata is higher than what it should be for *him*, as an individual. Therefore, he has vata vikruti.

Matty's Prakruti
{dosha balance he was born with}

vata   **pitta**   kapha

Matty's Vikruti
{dosha imbalance}

vata   **pitta**   kapha

the seven
dosha combinations

VATA

PITTA

KAPHA

VATA-PITTA*

PITTA-KAPHA

KAPHA-VATA

VATA-PITTA-KAPHA**

*it does not matter which dosha comes first. Vata-pitta and pitta-vata are considered the same.

**being tridoshic almost never happens.

Matty suddenly realizes he's not feeling, eating or sleeping well. A good little Ayurvedic student, he starts to make some adjustments. He incorporates a morning meditation and swaps-out his high-intensity exercise for yoga sessions. He also begins cooking meals at home again and brings his lunch to work, where he can warm it up. He takes regular short breaks during the day to restore energy and relieve his stress. Therefore he has a better focus on his job. Because he can focus, he feels more confident and happy and his stress levels decrease. Matty starts sleeping better and has a renewed sense of energy, alertness, focus and peace in his mind. The windy, high movement qualities have calmed down and his vata level goes back down.

This is where the understanding of each dosha is really important. We always work on balancing the vikruti first! Because Matty's vata was out of balance, he incorporated vata-balancing practices to bring him back to his prakruti of vata-pitta.

We always balance the vikruti first.

You know yourself better than anyone on the planet, so if you feel in your gut that something in your life needs to change or improve, you are probably right. Awareness is the first step in making a really impactful renaissance of self.

LIFE CHECK VIKRUTI

What are some things that may have caused your vikruti?

_____

_____

_____

_____

_____

_____

_____

_____

_____

_____

The qualities: gunas

We are now aware of our prakruti and vikruti (if you have it) and once we've got awareness, we need to know what to do with it. It is time to learn the gunas *(GOO-nuhz)* or qualities, so you can begin applying your awareness to the tangible. To bring us back to prakruti, we use the Ayurvedic rule "like increases like" which means the opposite qualities balance us. A simple example: if we are cold, we put on a sweater. If we are too hot, we remove layers. See? We already know when we need balance; we just need to give ourselves permission to listen to our instincts. Below are the 10 pairs of qualities in Ayurveda.

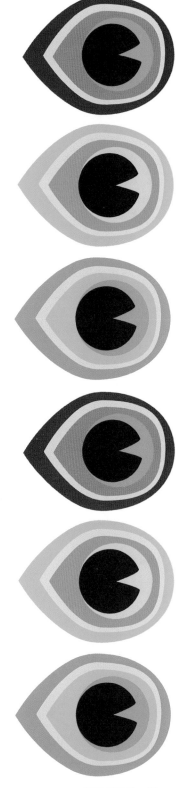

LIGHT ------------	HEAVY
COLD ------------	HOT
DRY ------------	WET/OILY
SOLID ------------	LIQUID
FAST ------------	SLOW
STATIC ------------	MOBILE
HARD ------------	SOFT
CLEAR ------------	CLOUDY
SMOOTH ------------	ROUGH
SUBTLE ------------	GROSS

Foods can be heavy, light, sticky. Seasons are cold, hot, wet. People can be heavy, light, cold and warm. Whenever my husband grabs my hand he says, "You are always so lovely and cool." And I say, "And you are always so toasty warm." In that way, we are a perfect balance! He needs my coolness and I need his hotness (hehe). Along the same lines, there are people who "light you up" and others who are "warm-hearted." The opposite could be true of people we might say "weigh us down" or come across as "cold."

Vata energy has a cold quality, so a vata person will have a tendency to be cold. If we gave them cold drinks and raw salads in winter, it would make them verrrrry *chitter-chatter* cold. They might get cold hands and feet or absent mindedness, constipation or moodiness. But what if we took that chilly 'lil vata in the winter and plopped them into a hot tub? They would get blissfully warm and the cold quality would instantly decrease. Vata heaven!

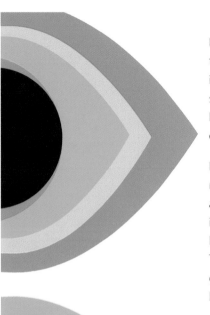

Pitta energy has a hot quality. If we gave a pitta person extra hot salsa with tortilla chips and a margarita white sitting in the hot sun, it would create an inferno inside their hot lil' body. They might get heart burn, red blotchy skin, irritability, or super sweaty and feel like they are going to pass out. Instead if we gave this lovely pitta a bowl of fresh fruit, a sun hat, and a glass of mint water, they would feel refreshed and calm.

Kapha energy has heavy and wet qualities. Let's say a kapha person is regularly eating mac 'n' cheese, bread bowls with creamy clam chowder, and fettuccine in cream sauce. The wet and heavy qualities in kapha would increase because of those foods. This kapha would gain weight, feel lethargic, may have increased mucus and feel an overall sense of heaviness. To balance, we could give them a variety of steamed vegetables with a light garlic-ginger sauce with a side of rice noodles and a spicy chai. They will feel light and energized.

The most powerful way to use this theory of opposites is to use it as a practice each day. The more often we collect "like" qualities around us, the more those qualities will build in excess which tips our doshic balance. Put on your memory cap and start to learn the qualities of the doshas.

VATA'S QUALITIES ARE: COLD, DRY, LIGHT, MOBILE, SUBTLE AND ROUGH

VATAS NEED: WARM, WET/OILY, HEAVY, STABLE, DENSE AND SMOOTH

PITTA'S QUALITIES ARE: HOT, SHARP, OILY, MOBILE AND SMOOTH

PITTAS NEED: COOL, DULL, DRY, STABLE AND ROUGH

KAPHA'S QUALITIES ARE: COLD, WET, HEAVY, STATIC, DENSE AND DULL

KAPHAS NEED: WARM, DRY, LIGHT, MOBILE, ROUGH AND SHARP

Which qualities do you notice in yourself?
How do they show up in your body-mind?

_____

_____

_____

_____

_____

_____

_____

_____

_____

List three people you love. What are their qualities?
What might their prakruti or vikruti be?

_____

_____

_____

_____

_____

_____

_____

_____

_____

_____

While you love them, they might drive you nuts from time to time.
How can you approach them with more compassion and understanding,
based on what you know about your dosha vs. their dosha?

_____

_____

_____

_____

_____

_____

ayur-tip

Along life's road, people may show up that we just don't "get" or may rub us the wrong way. The best thing we can do is respect them and honor their path. Instead of going to a place of judgement or frustration which are negative emotions that really only affect us, release them by sending a simple blessing. An example of a blessing is, "I don't really understand you or where you are coming from, but I bless and respect your outlook and unique contributions." Or, "Bless you. I really hope that life gets much better for you. I wish for you, a life that is full of what you love the most." Or, whatever the case may be, but I bet you could find something to send as a blessing for those people who you just don't jibe with. You are not only making life easier for yourself by acknowledging your separate paths in life, but at the same time, you are genuinely wishing the best for someone else.

4

IN-BALANCE

Balanced life

truth

The word balance means there are two+ forces acting at the same time, but they maintain equilibrium and proper function.

wisdom

Life ebbs and flows — it will forever change, so the goal is to stay balanced through all these ups, downs and hairpin turns of life.

Balanced vata creates energy. Balanced pitta creates radiance. Balanced kapha creates strength.

WHAT IS BALANCE

Work-life balance. Feeling balanced. Balancing life. Balancing work and kids. Balanced diet. Balancing finances. If you look at magazines in the check out line, I bet you could find one that mentions balance each time you're at the store. Everyone wants balance! But what exactly is balance? How do we know when we've achieved it? If I posed this question to ya'll in person, everyone would have a different definition of what balance means to them. But I tell you what would be common: the feeling around being balanced. We can feel when our body and mind are in harmony and peace. Flip side, we know when we are off kilter, even slightly.

Feeling imbalanced might include moodiness, frustration, exhaustion, anger, irritability, constipation, overly sweaty, scatter-brained, physical pains, lethargic and the list goes on. Ayurveda says listen to the body! We often ignore the subtle signs of imbalance in order to "power through" to the end. The problem is, there often is no end! So, then what? We can just power through the next day and the next and the next until we die or retire first? Boo. That ain't balance. Let's talk about what it means first and then what to do about it. If we understand what balance is and how we get imbalanced, it will prevent us from getting there in the first place and help us feel like sludge much less often.

Feeling "in balance'" is having equal health emotionally, mentally and physically. In Ayurveda, total balance means that your unique combination of space, air, fire, water, earth, stays the same throughout life as it did the day you were born. What was that word? Prakruti! Right on, smarties!

Optimal health is when your natural balance stays the same throughout life.

We maintain our balance through multiple methods including diet, daily routine, exercise, breathing techniques, the five senses, herbal therapies, even the company we keep! These are the life-blocks that create our most healthy foundation and from there we can flourish and grow upward. If one of these things is ignored, misused or misaligned, we will go out of balance.

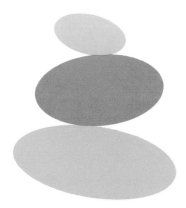

You'll need a pen, markers, or crayons for this next part! Many life or executive coaches (including mine) use the wheel below to see how well-rounded (literally!) your life is. Will yours be a smooth wheel or will you have a sore tushy from a bumpy ride? There is no judging so have fun and this should give you insights about your general life-balance. **INSTRUCTIONS:** Imagine the center of the wheel is 0 and the outer edge is 10. With your pen, color in your satisfaction in each pie shape, 0 being lowest, 10 being the highest. Color from the center to the number you choose. What areas need attention to ensure a smoother ride through your journey of life?

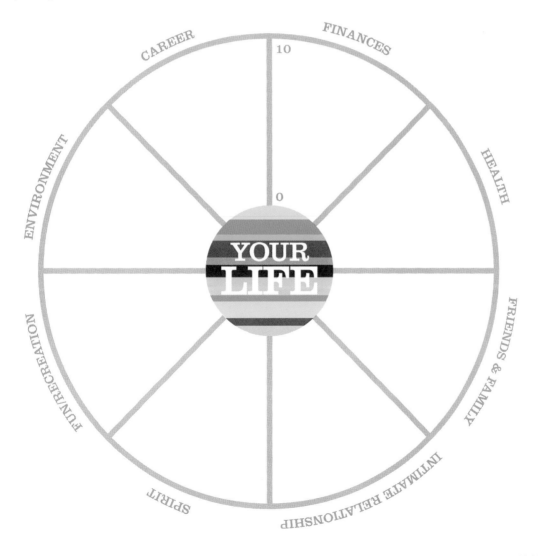

LIVE A BALANCED LIFE. LEARN SOME AND THINK SOME AND DRAW AND PAINT AND SING AND DANCE AND PLAY AND WORK EVERYDAY.

— **ROBERT FULGHUM**
All I really need to know I learned in kindergarten

What are your lowest areas in the wheel?

_____

_____

_____

_____

_____

What are two things you could do tomorrow to improve each area?

_____

_____

_____

_____

_____

Have you ever said that you feel "in your own skin" or "in your element"? Think back to times you have felt this way. When was that and what were you doing?

_____

_____

_____

_____

_____

_____

_____

_____

_____

_____

good stuff

When we are in that moment of, "Yessss…I am totally in my space, in my element, in my groove," that is balance and, dare I say, a moment of bliss! It is usually fleeting and might feel like a pause. The trick is to capture that moment, get into the groove and stay there as long as you can.

**This, my friend, is your recipe for happiness.
Do these things more!**

The things on this list make you feel awesome, in your groove, in your space, in your element. Yes! That feeling of being in your element is balance. Whether it's mental contentment or physical flow, we feel absolutely at home. Most of us have excellent radar when it comes to feeling balanced, we just have not had the license to trust ourselves. You know you better than *anyone* else, so listen to your body, your heart, your mind and your emotions. Permission granted to do often what makes you feel awesome.

In Ayurveda, imbalances are the result of only three categories

1) WRONG CHOICES, MISTAKEN INTELLECT
2) MISUSE OF THE SENSES
3) THE EFFECTS OF TIME

WRONG CHOICES

There is a wise, little part of our mind called buddhi *(boo-DEE)*. Buddhi is our inner wisdom, kind of like the "good angel" sitting on our shoulder whispering the right things to do in your ear. Our buddhi always helps us adhere to choices that would be best for us, whether big or small. When we listen to our buddhi we feel accomplished, are highly productive and are more likely to make the right choices by following through with right action.

If we do not listen to our budhhi, we will not make the right choices, which is the root cause of all kinds of problems. There's a waterfall effect for bad-choice-making because thing leads to another. Let's walk through two examples together 1) when we do not listen to our buddi and 2) when we do.

You did not listen to your buddhi

Let me be dramatic for a sec. After a wonderfully tantalizing meal, you are full, but the food was so good you want a second helping. Buddhi says, "One helping is enough or you will feel overfull." You know you don't need a second helping, but it was just so tasty! Against buddhi's advice, you have more food anyway. That second serving pushed you into a food coma and now you are too lethargic to take your 30-minute evening walk.

Instead, you veg in front of the TV watching *House Hunters*. You feel a bit disappointed in yourself and are irritated by small closets being a deal breaker, so you watch more TV (*Shark Tank*, anyone?) and you still feel very full. Since the TV is an addicting little bugger, you might stay up past your 10 p.m. Ayurvedic bedtime. As the night goes on, you get snacky. Buddhi says, "Don't do it! Just go to bed!" But you reach for the chocolates anyway because your sweet tooth is calling for it. Besides, you already screwed up the night so who cares. You get a sugar surge, so you stay up even later and have restless sleep because of the caffeine in the chocolates. You have a hard time waking up the next morning because your belly is still full from the night before. And then you wake up feeling like physical junk from too much food, guilt from watching too much TV and staying up too late. And all because you made the wrong choices — this was nobody else's fault.

The results of making wrong choices

You over ate and watched too much TV (drains energy and can cause insomnia). You stayed up too late. Your food was not digested properly — not digesting food thoroughly is the easiest way to gain weight and build-up toxins. Bummer.

Get my point? Wrong choices are responsible for SO many health problems. Let's start making better ones — it's totally in our control. Our wisdom is already there, we have it. It's just waiting for us to listen and act.

LIFE CHECK WRONG CHOICES

List examples of choices you make that you know are not good for you (be honest, nobody is judging).

_____

_____

_____

_____

_____

_____

_____

_____

What are the results of those wrong choices?

_____

_____

_____

_____

_____

_____

_____

_____

_____

_____

_____

_____

_____

_____

misusing the senses

- smoking
- very cold or very hot showers
- too much computer, TV or smart phone
- eating on the go
- eating too much
- eating foods that are too salty, too sugary, too tasty
- loud concerts
- the perfume section of a department store
- inhaling industrial fumes
- loud traffic
- loud construction noise
- not getting enough hugs
- driving while eating, drinking coffee and smoking while texting (highly dangerous, don't do it!)

You listened to your buddhi

Now let's say, you listened to your buddhi and only had one delicious helping at dinner. You felt physically nourished and had enough energy to clean up the kitchen and reward yourself by enjoying a leisurely evening walk outside at sunset. The walk refreshed you because you were out in nature able to enjoy some down time after a long day. Perhaps you even experienced something interesting on your walk, which may have sparked a nice conversation with a loved one when you got home. When there is downtime, our mind relaxes and we have pause. When we have pause, new ideas have a window to enter. Maybe you still watch *House Hunters* but limit to one episode because you know you can get sucked into TV for hours. After one episode, you have had your fill of small closets being a deal breaker and turn to a favorite book, knitting project, phone call to a friend or journal before bed.

The results of making right choices

Because you actually spent time nourishing yourself, you might have felt very good about how you spent your evening and therefore would actually want to go to sleep at 10 p.m.

> **We will not be perfect in our decision-making but at any time we derail, we can stop and make a better choice.**

Notice the difference of this scenario vs. the first one!? Like night and day! Each of your awesome choices influenced the next awesome choice. Once we start choosing and doing the right things, we will feel increasingly fabulous and we will want to do it more and more! However, the same happens if you make the wrong choices. It can easily end up in a domino effect of bad choices and then we feel like junk. We will not be perfect in our decision-making but at any time we derail, we can stop and make a better choice.

LIFE CHECK RIGHT CHOICES

List examples of when you listen to your buddhi.

_____

_____

_____

_____

_____

_____

What are the results of making these right choices?

_____

_____

_____

_____

_____

Great! Keep making those choices!

Now, look back at your wrong choices. Which ones will you commit to
changing? Start with one or two changes and build on those.

_____

_____

_____

_____

_____

MISTAKEN INTELLECT

Mistaken intellect simply means that we don't know what is good or bad
for us, so we make decisions with complete unknowing. It would be like
if we didn't understand gravity and we watched eggs roll off the counter.
Oops, we didn't know they would fall and smash! What a mess.
Ayurvedically-speaking, many folks will fall into this category because
we are just beginning to understand Ayurveda.

LIFE CHECK MISTAKEN INTELLECT

List some things you have learned in this book already that
you didn't know before.

_____

_____

_____

_____

_____

_____

_____

MISUSE OF THE SENSES

The five senses are our only connection and interpretation of information to the physical world. Everything we experience in our life is realized through the senses of sight, sound, touch, taste and smell. Our senses are the vehicles Ayurveda uses for healing in various therapies to bring the body back into proper balance. Because activating and treating the senses can actually heal us, any misuse of the senses can greatly imbalance us, too. When the senses are fed too much, too little, or wrong information, they deliver it to the body and mind. Then things can get really screwy.

Let's be dramatic again for a second. Imagine Las Vegas. The Strip. You walk into a casino and *BINGLE JINGLE JANGLE BING BING BING* You are suddenly smacked in the ears with loud jingling, bingling sounds from the machines. The room is full of smoke and to cover it up, there is super stinky air perfume pumped into the room. Double stinky whammy. Thousands of electronic screens with flashy fun animated things flicker and dance to keep you engaged for hours as people serve you bottomless drinks. Oh, and they pump in oxygen, too. Um. SENSORY OVERLOAD!

For our delicate and highly intelligent senses this is just way too much to digest all at once. Good thing they have spas and massages in Vegas to bring that shizz back to balance! Treat your senses with great care and respect. They are the vehicles that deliver all kinds of wonderful information to our bodies to help us experience and absorb the world around us. If you feel like your senses have been abused or neglected, give them some reprieve, give them a refresher and nourishment. There will be much more detail on the senses in chapter 11.

THE EFFECTS OF TIME

We can control so many aspects of our health, but time is not one of them. We cannot control our age, when the seasons change or how fast the clock moves. However, we can make decisions that navigate our boat smoothly through the waves of time.

Time changes us as we age. We go from being chubby babies and toddlers to energetic kids to opinionated teens to working, goal-oriented adults to golden-aged to wise elderly folk. We would not expect an elderly person to be as physical active or resilient as a teenager, nor would we expect a teenager to be as wise as someone in their golden years.

The seasons are transformative and require us to adapt. The effect of winter tells us to add more clothes and eat comforting heavy foods. It also tells us to put more moisture on our skin because winter is very dry. In contrast, the effect of summer tells us to wear lighter clothes and take a dip in the pool to stay cool.

Time also changes every second of every day. The sun rises and sets at a different time each day. When it's dark at 5 p.m. in winter, we feel like going to bed earlier than when the sun sets at 9:30 p.m. in summer — the effect of time is putting us to sleep or keeping us awake. Our awareness around how time affects us is key to living a healthy Ayurvedic lifestyle.

LIFE CHECK EFFECTS OF TIME

Give examples of how the effects of time has changed you:

_____

_____

_____

_____

_____

_____

_____

_____

_____

_____

In the next chapter, we will look at how doshas rule time and what we can do to live in harmony with the daily routine, the seasons and our age. Let the fun continue!

5
LIFE-TIME

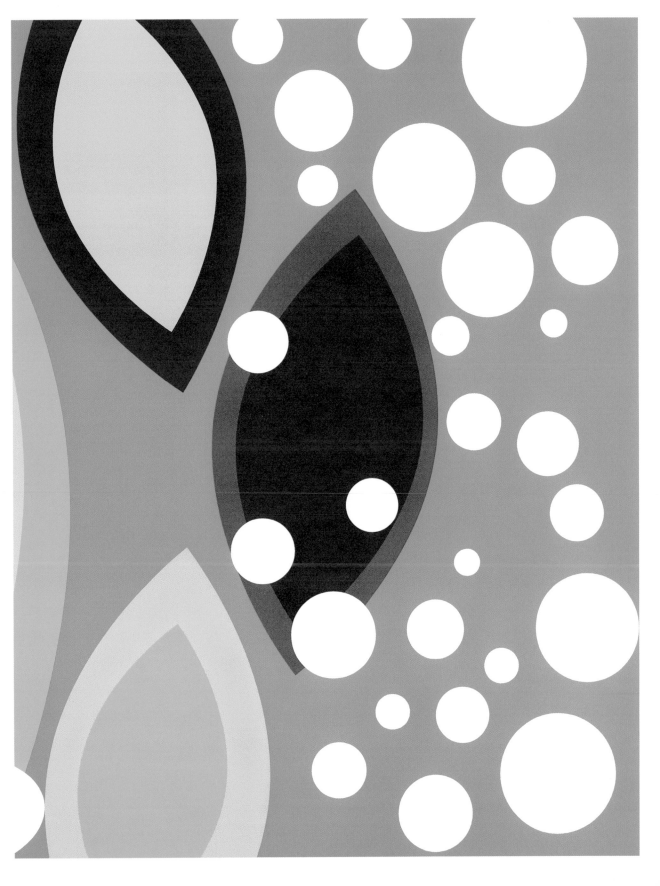

Timing is everything

In Ayurveda, timing is everything because ideally we should follow nature's clock. Following nature's clock is the daily routine or dinacharya *(DIN-na-CHAR-ya),* and it is the corner stone of Ayurvedic preventative medicine.

Every day there is a time for the sun to rise and a time for the stars to peek out. Every day, like clockwork, it happens. In fact, we are awake during the day because the sun tells us to "wake up!," be active and go be productive. When the sun goes down, it is a signal for us to sleep. We rely on waking up in the morning and sleeping at night as a consistent schedule. What varies is how closely *we* match what nature is doing.

Can I share a story about time? In college, I used to wake up at what I called "the crack" or, 5:30 a.m. to go to the gym. What college kid does that? Right. It was only because the gym was empty and I had my choice of any machine I wanted, which made my pitta (competition) and vata (space-needing) very happy. Here's where I fell apart: I would come back to the dorm around 7 a.m. and go back to sleep until 9 a.m., which meant I skipped my 8 a.m. Geology 101 class (don't tell my mom!). I hated it anyway but the kicker was that I was totally sluggish for my art class at 11 a.m., which I loved. Had I known the rules about nature's clock, I would have known that going back to sleep was the worst thing I could do for my energy.

Most of us are oblivious to nature's clock (mistaken intellect), but because we are part of nature, we should flow with its schedule. It is most important to know the best time to eat, sleep, exercise, meditate and so on. Once we start to jibe with this flow, we start to feel amazing and effortlessly slide back into balance. Many of the health complaints we have might start to disappear or lessen once we start jamming to the tune of nature.

The Ayurvedic daily routine will help you flush out not only what times are best for specific activities but *why* times are best for specific activities. We will also go through the Ayurvedic seasonal routine and the Ayurvedic lifetime routine.

---

dinacharya

Dinacharya is preventative medicine by following the daily routine according to nature's clock. A few more details on the order of dinacharya are below:

- Wake up before sunrise

- Say a prayer or write a list of 10 things you are grateful for

- Wash your face, eyes and mouth (scrape tongue, brush teeth)

- Drink a glass of water

- Poop

- Swish with sesame oil in your mouth for a few minutes and spit

- Abhyanga, full body oil massage (p. 200)

THE AYURVEDIC DAILY ROUTINE

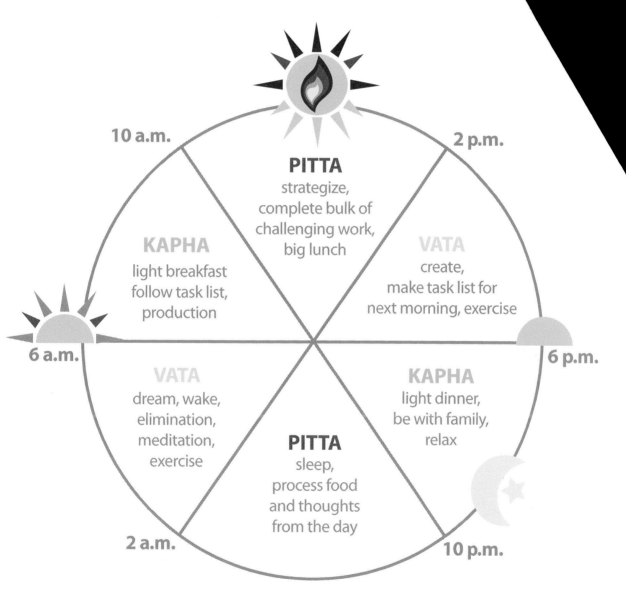

PITTA
strategize,
complete bulk of
challenging work,
big lunch

KAPHA
light breakfast
follow task list,
production

VATA
create,
make task list for
next morning, exercise

VATA
dream, wake,
elimination,
meditation,
exercise

KAPHA
light dinner,
be with family,
relax

PITTA
sleep,
process food
and thoughts
from the day

10 a.m.

2 p.m.

6 a.m.

6 p.m.

2 a.m.

10 p.m.

ᴠ! The daily routine is one of the easiest places to start when trying to
the wrinkles in our habits and routine. The daily routine is based on
that govern certain times of day and once you understand it,
art incorporating the routine right away. This is where your
the doshas and their qualities come in handy.

Kapha time. The energy of kapha is slow and steady.
un coming up over the horizon. Once the sun is up,
ᴇ, which means the energy in nature is very heavy. When we
ᴏᴏ long, it's hard to wake up. If we sleep until after the sun is up, we
are rising in the energy of kapha heaviness, which will give a sluggish start to
the day. Because the energy is heavy, we should eat a light breakfast around
7 or 7:30 a.m. with just enough food to tide us over until lunch. In the morning,
our agni (*AHG-nee*) is just waking up, too, so we can support it by rekindling it
with a warm breakfast to make sure it's strong enough for lunch. Kapha time
is great for getting things done! Because kapha energy is a "follower," it feels
good to sit down and follow a task list we created the day before. Think about
it, when we first get to work, we are not feeling ultra-creative or ready to tackle
heavy strategy, right? What if, instead, we could follow a simple task list and
get a bunch of work crossed off the 'to-do' list first thing in the morning?
Sign me up! Kapha will help you stick to and complete that list. Productivity
at its best!

10 a.m. – 2 p.m. Pitta time. Who feels like they need a snack around 10 a.m.?
Ha! Most people do. That's because agni has digested breakfast so now the
fire is getting bigger. Agni says "I'm hungry!" which means it is setting us up
nicely to hit our digestive peak at noon. Remember, we are a part of nature
and all the fires are in alignment at noon. Agni (little fire in us) and pitta (fire
in us and in nature) relate to the sun (biggest fire in nature) and the sun is the
strongest it will be all day. Therefore our agni is strongest at noon, too.

In conjunction with our digestion doing a lot of work, our brain will also
want to do a lot of work from 10 a.m. to 2 p.m. This is the best time to strategize,
make new goals, problem-solve, organize and analyze. Pitta governs and
transforms thoughts, perceptions, discriminations, and intellect. So pitta's
energy will help you do all those tasks best at that time.

2 p.m. – 6 p.m. Vata time. At about 2 or 3 p.m., we might start feeling a
little antsy…we might start jonesin' for a snack, a coffee or tea break, or the
urge to jibber-jabber with coworkers. Sound familiar? That's vata energy
wanting to move. We're probably not really hungry, but we might snack
because we're sick of sitting around and our mind wants to day dream
about…mmm, snacks. If we have afternoon meetings we likely won't be

sunrise will give a
ᴊɪsh start to your day. Flip
side, waking up even 10–15
minutes before sunrise will give
you a boost of energy and will
stay with you the entire day!

Eat lunch close to noon and
make it your biggest meal.

Dinner should be small, about
half the quantity of lunch so that
you can digest it fully before bed.

Kapha time at night is to unwind,
not add more grind.

able to pay attention and will have doodle-scribbles on our notes. Ride with it! This is a great time to create and innovate. Creative meetings and creative work should be done at this time of day. One of the best tips when vata is tossing all kinds of ideas into our head is to write it down and make a task list for the next morning. Boom! Watch what happens next…you'll love it. Not only will this help capture ideas so we don't get overwhelmed, but this is the list you will love to have when you get to work during kapha time in the morning.

6 p.m. – 10 p.m. Kapha time. After we get home from work, it's not time for computer or more work, it's time to relax. Kapha loves food and family love. Kaphas love to have leisure time and take it slooooow. Speaking of slow, our agni starts to slow way down, too. Unless it's summer, there is no more sunlight. After 6 p.m. when the fire in the sky goes down, our agni does, too. Have a light dinner. It's time for family, relaxation, nurturing, hobbies and winding down. Heavy kapha energy will also help put us to sleep, so it is important to get to bed by 10 p.m. before pitta time kicks in.

10 p.m. – 2 a.m. Pitta time. If we stay up past 10 p.m. we might feel a "second wind." We might start rehashing the day's problems and relive frustrations about whatever was bugging us earlier. We might even get a sudden urge to scrub the burners and organize the sock drawer by color. Ever have that happen? Suddenly we aren't tired anymore! Well, that's pitta kicking back in. Pitta digests and transforms all thoughts, perceptions, foods — everything given to our mind and body from the entire day. Pitta usually sneaks around doing the transforming while we sleep (like a magic fairy) but if we stay up much past 10 p.m., it will transform all that stuff while we are awake. No stopping nature, it's moving on with or without our cooperation. This transformation is extremely important as it goes towards rejuvenating all gastrointestinal tract organs/biological processes if one is asleep. That's why staying up too late is a common root cause of digestive orders! Lesson? Bed by tennypoo! Let pitta do its transformation while we rest, it doesn't need our help. The socks drawer is just fine semi-rumpled.

2 a.m. – 6 a.m. Vata time. At this time, we're still sleeping, but the body is preparing itself to wake and start moving. Dreams start happening, there is movement in the colon (vata rules colon!) preparing for elimination, and our mind is the closest to our spirit, or higher self. It's a prime time for spirituality and meditation. Ideally we should wake up before sunrise so that we rise with vata's energy of movement. We could also exercise at this time of day because we will get moving easily. This will improve our energy level for the entire day! So, wake up, go to the bathroom (ideally poop), drink water and do yoga and/or meditation. You will have eliminated all the stuff that pitta

ayur-tips

Set your strategy and "thinkey" meetings at work during the 10–2 time slot (but don't skip lunch) because people are at their sharpest and ready for a challenge during pitta time.

At 4 p.m., write a task list for the next morning. That way when you start your day in kapha, you will know exactly what to do — you will have the list to follow.

Ayurvedic classic texts say that waking up 48 minutes before sunrise is the optimal time to practice "whatever one wants to do successfully for the rest of their life."

digested and ready to start a new day fresh with new choices, new challenges and a nice task list waiting on your desk. Yes, I'm still talkin' about that task list. Cause it's awesome!

Ever wake up around 2 or 3 a.m. and are unable to fall asleep again until sunrise? Yepper, there's a reason! If we wake during vata time, vata energy can keep us awake especially if vata is high or imbalanced. Then just when the sun creeps above the horizon, we start feeling heavy, like we could sleep for days. That's a perfect example of where the doshas meet each other in time.

YOUR CURRENT ROUTINE

Now that you know what the recommended Ayurvedic daily routine is, let's find out how closely you match it. As a reminder, this book is a "judgement-free" zone. We are not striving for perfection, we are striving for improvement. Let's just see where you are now compared to the Ayurvedic routine.

Ready!? Fill in approximately what your current daily schedule looks like. Just write it on the lines. This includes everything you do each day like wake up, exercise, meals, commute, work/meetings, lesure and bed time. **HINT:** If you're thinking, "Um, my schedule changes daily," that means this is a great opportunity to make it more reliable and balanced by nature.

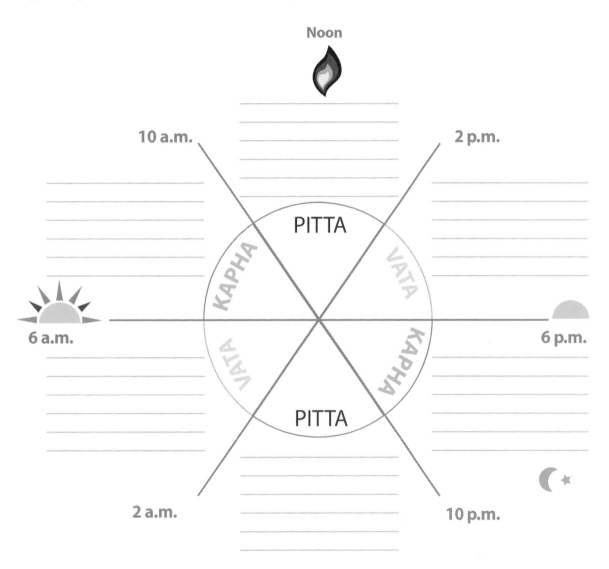

Compare. Take a look at the Ayurvedic routine (p. 75). How does yours match up? I'm sure some parts are in line with nature and others need to be adjusted. Perhaps you just need to rotate your entire schedule an hour or so to line up. Take note because on the next page, you will make a new schedule to be more in line with the Ayurvedic one.

Alrighty! Here's your chance to make your routine healthier for you. Now, make a new routine with the goal to make it more Ayurvedic (again, reference p. 75). Feel free to completely change your schedule, but keep it realistic. For example, if you are never going to exercise at 6:30 a.m., don't put that on here as a lofty goal.. Set yourself up for success and see how close you can get!

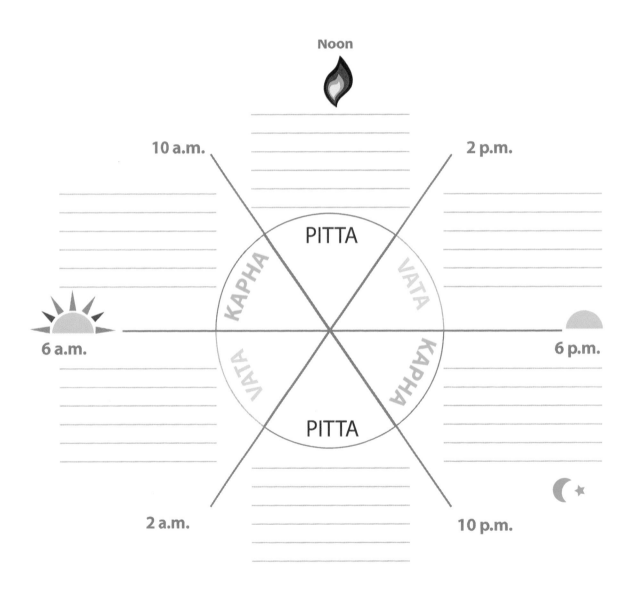

Look at that beautiful stuff! Without even turning your world upside-down, you are able to live much closer to nature's rhythm. If you want to get started right away, choose two changes to incorporate. Or, you can wait to compile everything when we bring it all together in chapter 14.

LIFE CHECK YOUR NEW ROUTINE

Date: /   /

Two changes you are committing to:

_____

_____

_____

_____

Results one week later:

_____

_____

_____

_____

Results two weeks later:

_____

_____

_____

_____

Results four weeks later:

_____

_____

_____

_____

I'm so excited and I'm going to add two more changes!

_____

_____

_____

_____

YOU CAN KEEP ADDING CHANGES AND TRACKING
YOUR PROGRESS IN A JOURNAL, ON COMPUTER,
DIGITAL CALENDAR, IN A BLOG OR SHARE SUCCESSES
WITH ME AND I'LL PUT THEM ON **HEYMONICAB.COM**.

psst...are you sleeping?

two types of insomnia

1) Not being able to fall asleep: a pitta problem caused by high stress.

2) Waking up in the middle of the night and not being able to fall back to sleep: a vata problem often caused by anxiety and a racing mind.

Vatas are particularly sensitive to lack of sleep. They will quickly feel the imbalance including increased anxiety, insomnia, unable to handle stress, over- eating or under-eating and extreme mood swings.

LIFESTYLE TIPS FOR GETTING GOOD Z'S

- In bed by 10 p.m.
- Stick to the daily routine. Your day ends with sleep so if everything else is in line, your sleep will fall in line as well.
- Don't eat too much, too late. Not good for many reasons, but heart burn or indigestion is uncomfortable and can keep us awake.
- Practice daily pranayama (p. 165). Do so hum (p. 166) or nadi shodhanam (p. 167) daily! Start with 5 minutes. Great for calming the nerves (vata) and the mind (pitta).
- Do oil massage, a.k.a. abhyanga (ah-bee-YOUNG-guh p. 200) daily.
- No caffeine after noon. Limiting caffeine in general is best, but if you have coffee, keep it to the morning hours only.
- Exercise regularly. A 30-minute daily walk is perfect for almost everyone.

IN A PINCH IF YOU ARE TOSSING AND TURNING

- Add a sprinkle of cardamom and nutmeg to a small glass of warm milk and drink.
- Massage adhipati (ah-DEE-pah-TEE) marma (MAR-muh) which is an energy point on the top of our head — it's the soft spot on babies. The point is eight finger-widths away from the eyebrows, on top of the head. Place four fingers across the forehead, edge of the pinkie touching the eyebrows. Take your other hand and stack another four fingers on top of those. Remove your first hand and use your index finger to find the point at the edge of your hand in the middle of the head. Massage clockwise with the middle finger 1–2 minutes.
- Massage your kirkatika (Kur-KAH-teeka) marma. Easier this time. It's the point where your neck meets your spine at the back of the head where there is an indentation. Massage clockwise with middle finger 1–2 minutes.
- Lay on your right side and do so hum.

aaaand...goodnight.

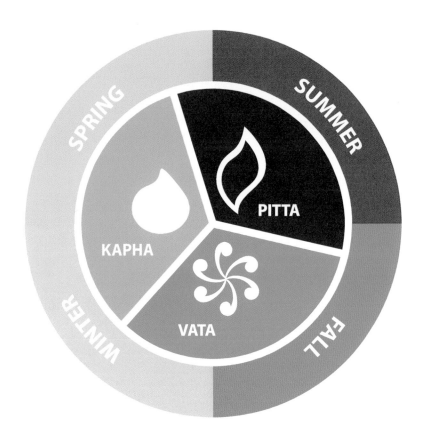

resource

Years back I made three free **Seasonal Bloom** booklets for each season. They are still on my site for free download.

Go to **heymonicab.com** and search *"Seasonal Bloom."*

THE SEASONS

While doshas rule certain times of day, they also rule the seasons and we respond accordingly. We do not turn into different doshas just because the seasons change. Our doshic balance stays the same, but if our dosha matches the season, there's a strong likelihood we'll get imbalanced/overflowed with that dosha. We are already balancing ourselves during the seasons in so many ways. For example, when it's raining, we use an umbrella to keep dry. When it's hot outside, we sweat to release excess internal heat. We apply moisturizer as our skin gets a little more dry in fall and winter. Let's get a deeper understanding of how the doshas influence the seasons and ultimately our behavior.

The chart above shows where the doshas fall into play during the year. Notice there are only three doshas that overlap four seasons.

VATA SEASON: FALL THROUGH EARLY WINTER

Fall through early winter is vata season. The outside air cools down, becomes "crisp" and less humid. Leaves dry up, fall off and get crunchy. Think about a dry crispy leaf flipping around in the breeze — a perfect example of vata energy. The sun shines for fewer hours during the day resulting in less light and less heat. We begin putting on extra layers, like maybe a vest or warmer jacket. At the mercy of nature, we get dry skin, static in our hair and our hands and toes get cold easily. We also might feel a little in the dumps because of the lack of sun. On a deeper level vata-types might experience "unexplained" anxiety, panic, worry, constipation, pain in our joints, headaches, mood swings and an overall feeling of ungroundedness. This is all due to the over-arching energy of vata affecting our minds and bods.

Vata season: eat

To counterbalance the crisp, wispy chill in the air outside, we need to eat foods like thick soups, stews, veggie chilli, sweet potatoes, root vegetables, noodle dishes. Plenty of water is important so the body doesn't dry out but the real key is to eat plenty of healthy oils to keep our insides "buttered." Oils nourish the brain to enhance focus and concentration and can boost our mood. Not to mention, oils keep vatas regular!

DURING VATA SEASON, WE NEED:
WARM AND GROUNDING COMFORT FOODS,
A RELIABLE SCHEDULE IN ACCORDANCE
WITH THE DAILY ROUTINE, EXERCISES THAT
PROVIDES GROUNDING AND BREATHWORK.

Vata season: schedule

There is not any real magic behind a vata's schedule except to follow the Ayurvedic daily routine and keep it reliable. Vatas should make it a habit to do the same routine each day. Not only does it hold them in a structure, but it calms their mind so they don't have to constantly think about what is next. Sleep is crucial for all doshas but especially for vata. One of the quickest ways to imbalance a vata is to screw up their sleep schedule.

Vata season: exercise

Vatas need to take it slow, be mindful, and stay grounded while they are exercising in the winter. Too much movement, jumping, catching air and whirling around will increase those qualities in them and that's already happening outside. We want to ground vata by throwing a 50 pound sack of warm rice on their back to slow them down. Just kidding. But it's kind of like that. Vatas will do best when both feet stay on the ground like yoga, barre/ballet routine, and light weight-lifting. If the exercise is too rigorous, fast, bouncy or kinetic, vatas will create a tizzy and exercise will actually imbalance them, rather than providing benefit.

KAPHA SEASON: LATE WINTER THROUGH LATE SPRING

Kapha season is spring and the time for creation. During late winter and early spring, the snow that falls is a bit wetter and heavier than it was in early winter. We are now blessed with extra rain so as nature unthaws, grass can grow, trees can bud and flowers can bloom. That is kapha's job! Kapha nourishes, nurtures, protects, builds and creates, giving bounty and beauty to all of the surrounding nature (and us). It's natural to feel a "spring" in our step and a need to lighten the load. Kaphas are heavy by nature but feel their best when they get rid of stuff (emotions included) that no longer serves them. This is why spring cleaning feels so awesome!

We start to dethaw from winter as our skin starts to plump up and we might be refreshed by dampness in the air or some rainfall. We might go outside to take deep inhales and capture some of the fresh prana in the air. We get a glimmer of warmer days ahead as the bitter chill has been taken out of the air and we might get a little cabin fever as we itch to get outdoors. As kapha begins to accumulate, we might have extra mucus in our chest or noses, allergies might creep in and we might get a spring cold or congestion. Deeper imbalances might include ezcema, joint pain, arthritis and swelling.

Kapha season: eat

In spring, we crave renewal as we spring clean our homes and start eating lighter foods. We might choose a dietary spring cleanse to reduce stagnation from winter to refresh our bodies and minds. It is still cool and damp outside, so the best foods for kapha season are light, dry, spicy and warm. Some examples are spicy brothy soups, asian-inspired dishes with a ginger spice combo, rice noodle dishes or spicy stir fried vegetables over rice. Puffed foods are especially great, like popcorn. Foods should not be iced, raw or too cold because kapha is trying to thaw. If kapha does not thaw and liquify, it turns into sticky mucus goo and we get extra congestion.

> DURING KAPHA SEASON, KAPHAS NEED: WARM AND DRY FOODS, REDUCTION IN MATERIAL POSESSIONS, WARM SPICY TEAS, AND INVIGORATING EXERCISE TO INCREASE HEAT FROM THE INSIDE OUT.

Kapha season: schedule

Kaphas stick to the daily schedule but have to be mindful not to sleep too much. Too much sleep is kapha aggravating and will cause them to be even more lethargic. No naps! Instead, pick an extra activity that makes your body move, whether it's gardening, a morning walk or a new class at the gym with your favorite buddy.

---

tips that may help relieve SAD

Seasonal Affective Disorder (SAD) is a perfect example of how nature is our energetic umbrella. We can't change the seasons, so we have to change ourselves. Here are some things that may relieve SAD.

- Omega-3 fats and oils internally
- Daily warm oil massage
- Fireplaces and candles
- Limit refined sugars and alcohol (hello…depressant)
- Write a list of 20 things you are grateful for, daily
- Plan a week-long vacation between January and April
- Short bursts of exercise will increase prana and heat
- Apply aromatherapy on wrists, drop on the floor of the shower, add to baths, or add in a diffuser
- Sit in a warm bath, hot tub, steam room or sauna
- Buy fresh cut flowers or plant bulbs in a colorful pot indoors
- Play upbeat tunes that make you feel like you are on vacation in a warm destination
- Take classes in something you love. It gives us something to look forward to each week.
- Be with friends, family and loved ones. Our hearts light up when we have love in our life.

Kapha season: exercise

While kapha dosha is static, don't forget that kapha is also creation and rejuvenation. Kapha is a builder (creates structure) and when it's ready to rebuild after the dead of winter — or "dread of winter" as my mid-Western friends call it — nature needs to move and sprout, therefore so do we. Exercise feels refreshing after a long winter. The best exercise for kapha is cardio — kaphas need to move and sweat! Sweat gets rid of excess water which is good because extra water can make kapha feel heavier. The heat will help them feel lighter and will increase their otherwise sluggish and damp digestive fire. Exercise for kaphas should be fun, with a buddy and include lots of movement!

PITTA SEASON: LATE SPRING THROUGH EARLY FALL

Late spring through early fall is pitta season. The weather warms up and gets more humid, while the sun is hotter and the days are longer. The sun is pitta as heat increases outside and therefore heat in us increases! Humidity and heat outdoors causes us to sweat more and crave cooling drinks and foods. The huge, bright pitta in the sky (the sun) shines for a much longer period of time as the days get longer.

Because nature is warming up, we sweat more, our hair gets a little greasier, we might get skin blemishes or sunburn, and we feel more energy with a desire to be outside. On a deeper level, pitta-types are more prone to heating problems like heartburn, acid reflux, rashes, red itchy eyes, irritability, even hot tempers and short fuses — this time of year more than any other.

> **DURING PITTA SEASON, PITTAS NEED:**
> COOLING AND SOOTHING FRESH FOODS, PROTECTION FROM THE SUN, COOL WATER, COOLING AND STRESS-RELIEVING ACTIVITIES.

Pitta season: eat

As nature's way of balancing us, we will crave cooling drinks like fruit juices, mint water and iced tea. We gravitate towards fresh seasonal fruits, salads and the occasional ice cream or gelato. These fresh foods cool down and balance the heat from the outside. Pitta people specifically will easily overheat and will likely drink lots of extra water to keep them cool. Coconut water and pomegranate juice are also excellent for pitta.

Pitta season: schedule

Yes, it will stay lighter longer in the evening but that doesn't mean we should work into the wee hours (I know you, pittas) because that will make pittas crabby. Follow the Ayurvedic routine and find some time slots for extra enjoyment. Balancing pitta means "chilling out," enjoying downtime, not using the extra daylight to squeeze in more work.

---

ayur-tip

Walking with bare feet in cool grass is especially cooling for pittas and provides relief for hot, itchy eyes.

Pitta season: exercise

The weather could not be better to encourage pittas to enjoy some R&R outdoors. During pitta season, we get a refreshing change by being able to use all of the outdoors for exercise. We could take a dip in the pool, the lake or the ocean in lieu of the gym. Evening walks when the sun is setting is a perfect way for a pitta to relieve stresses and cool down for the day. A word of caution is never exercise during pitta time (between 10 a.m. and 2 p.m.). This can easily overheat pitta causing lightheatedness or even passing out from sun exposure. The sun + pitta time + pitta person = too much heat!

LIFE CHECK SEASONS

What new things did you learn about adjusting to each seasons? What is one thing you can you try right now, in this season?

Vata season adjustments:

_____

_____

_____

_____

Pitta season adjustments:

_____

_____

_____

_____

Kapha season adjustments:

_____

_____

_____

_____

ritusandhi

Ritusandhi (RIT-oo-SAHN-dee) is the joint between seasons. Transitioning between seasons is when we tend to get sick. Our bodies have been used to the routine, food and lifestyle of the last season and without some prep work, switching to a new season immediately affects our immunity. Simple guidelines to keep you healthy during ritusandhi:

- Do a kitchari cleanse (p.203) for 5 days to rid toxins and rebuild the body-mind with renewed cells and tissues

- This is a great time for panchakarma (p. 207)

- Incorporate foods that are appropriate for the upcoming season while weaning off foods from the last season

- Adjust your exercise routine if necessary to balance with the season. Slow down in fall/winter. Speed up in spring. Cool down in summer.

- Be diligent with the daily routine

- Keep your dosha in mind

KAPHA

birth

puberty

PITTA

adulthood

menopause

VATA

senior

death

Doshas rule the day, they rule the seasons and they also rule the stages of life. Kapha stage of life is creation. Pitta stage of life is change. Vata stage of life is destruction.

Conception through adolescence is kapha life cycle.

Kapha life cycle

From conception through childhood is our kapha life cycle. That means the overarching energy for our life at that time is kapha. Kapha is the energy of lubrication and structure, therefore it creates and builds. When we are a tiny cell growing into a rapidly growing human being, that is kapha. When we are born super soft, clear-eyed and need a lot of sleep, that is kapha. Babies and toddlers are chubby, they fall down, tumble, and are resilient to injury. They can go and go and go without getting tired which is the stamina of kapha. They are sweet, have cute little round angel faces and are still in fast growth mode until about puberty. Kapha life cycle is all about creation, growth, stability and learning.

Adolescence through menopause is pitta life cycle.

Pitta life cycle

Adolescence through menopause (generally in our 50s, but it depends on the person), is our pitta life cycle. When puberty hits it's, "What happened to my sweet kid?!" We don't grow as much from puberty to adulthood as we did from an itty bitty, miniscule cell to a teen. We have more opinions, our own objections, agendas, and want to achieve goals OUR way. We are more competitive whether in sports, academics, with friends, about clothes, make up and cliques. Pitta will show up in our suddenly gung-ho personalities, but also on the skin as some teens get acne or pimples. We eat a lot in quantity and seem to have endless hunger. Usually the choice is junk or fast-foods because we can make our own choices and the ego (me-me-me) starts to take over. There is no wisdom yet because we have not been on Earth for very long, but we look like adults and jockey to define our role in family, friends and the start of our own life.

For about the next 30 years we are in pitta life cycle. Striving, executing, achieving, goal-setting, working hard, being measured, measuring ourselves and a lot of go-go-go, strive-strive-strive are all attributes of pitta.

Once we hit menopause age, pitta starts to leave the body and we enter vata life cycle.

Vata life cycle

Vata life cycle arrives in our 50s and lasts until our bodies expire. We begin reflecting on what our life has been and may have a different perspective now. We have stories about mistakes we've made, lessons we've learned, and what we are proud of. Reflecting on our action-filled time during pitta life cycle, we've gained wisdom and no longer sweat the small stuff. We live closer to our heart vs. our ego. Our skin gets thinner and loses elasticity (elasticity is kapha). Our memory might start to fade, our hair turns coarse instead of silky, and our bodies become more delicate. Because we have much less heat than pitta life cycle, we eat less, might have some constipation (prune juice anyone?) and our muscles start losing their tone and strength. Our body is moving towards a cataboloic state which means it starts to break down and dry out. What enhances is our subtle wisdom and connection to the spirit, the higher self.

Yay! Now you know all about nature's clock by the day, by the season and by life cycle. As we march along to nature's harmony, we have to accept and adjust to all that is out of our control. In that, we find our own balance and peace.

LIFE CHECK   THE ONES YOU LOVE

List some people you love and the life stage they are in. How can you offer more balance and/or loving kindness as they move through their stage?

_____

_____

_____

_____

_____

_____

_____

_____

_____

_____

learn

Kapha is anabolic — construction and building.

Pitta maintains.

Vata is catabolic — breaks things down, deteriorates.

nature

To sprout a seedling, we put it in the earth and water it. That is the start of creation, which is kapha. The seed needs sun and water, which transforms the seed into a sprout, and that is pitta. Once sprouted it turns into a leafy plant. When the plant gets older, it gets spindly and brittle, which is the energy of vata. The life cycle of a plant is the same as ours.

6
FIRE-WORKS

AGNI

Our digestive fire

The body's internal digestive fire (metabolism) is called our agni. When agni functions properly, whatever we have eaten gets digested and absorbed by the body. The body uses what it needs and then eliminates the rest as waste. However, when doshas are imbalanced due to lifestyle, diet, negative emotions, etc., agni becomes weakened or disturbed and cannot function properly. Most disease and imbalance is caused by malfunctioning agni, so it's important to know what it is and how it is supposed to work.

> **Most disease and imbalance is caused by malfunctioning agni.**

THE STORY OF AGNI

Visualize agni as a little burning flame behind our belly buttons. In the morning, agni is just waking up and pretty small (envision: teeny little cute flame, yawning, blinking eyes with outstretched arms). The goal is to help agni grow bigger. If we wake up hungry, we want to give agni just a little something warm to work on because agni is not ready for a heavy breakfast. It's too little. A big meal at this time would squish agni and put it right out! Let's think of the small, warm breakfast as kindling. Kindling makes a small fire grow larger! If we put a log (bacon, eggs, hash browns, orange juice, pancakes) on a small fire, what happens? The fire goes out. If we are hungry, we should have a small breakfast which is manageable for agni to digest so that it can grow.

AGNI STARTS GROWING...

By 10 a.m. when pitta energy kicks in, we might feel a little snacky. That is because pitta, the sun, and agni are all getting stronger, which makes us hungry. The goal is to have a nice raging agni fire by noon. At noon we should eat our biggest meal of the day so agni has the rest of the day to digest it. Because agni is strong at this time, it can handle a bunch of work.

As the afternoon goes on, agni is working hard on digesting our big lunch. At the same time, the sun is getting lower in the sky. By dinner time, agni is not only tired, but does not have power and heat like it did at noon. This is why Ayurveda says to eat a small dinner. Once the sun goes down, the heart closes like a lotus flower and the normal functions of the body reduce. Therefore, agni curls up with a blankie and rests for the evening. When it wakes up the next day, the cycle starts over again.

WHERE OUR WESTIE SCHEDULES GO WRONG

1) We skip breakfast or have a cold, raw smoothie. Or yogurt with fruit. Fire can't grow if we throw cold goop on it!
2) We eat a light lunch like a salad. Agni needs substantial fuel to get us through the rest of the day and a small salad ain't enough.
3) Because lunch was tiny, we are starving by the time we get home so we inhale a big dinner and go to sleep.

The problem? With a large meal at night and a shrinking agni, the big dinner will sit in our guts, undigested, until agni has enough energy to work on it again the next day. Most people will eat breakfast on top of that undigested food which makes it twice as hard for agni. Over time, this creates an old food pile that never gets processed. With all that undigested food, we're quickly on the road to weight gain and ama (toxins you will learn about shortly). Brightside! With simple commitment this can all be changed.

Give agni a lot to work on at noon, yes! But give agni a lot to work on in the evening and, um, no bueno.

Let me give you a real life example. At our jobs, we complete the bulk of our work during the day. Imagine if we came home at night to find even more work than we've had all day, to be completed between 7–10 p.m. We would be like, "Forget this." And we would quit before we start — it's just too much to accomplish in a short amount of time. Agni feels the same way about having to digest (work!) too much food that late in the day.

ayur-tip

Agni is a small amount of sun in our bodies, therefore agni rises and sets with the sun. When the sun is out, agni is more ready to digest food than when the sun is down. That's why we should not eat too much late at night because there is nothing left to digest our food.

Balanced agni is the root of a healthy life.

However, we could do some light tasks like dishes, laundry, light reading, and respond to personal emails. Those light tasks for us is what a light dinner is to agni. Totally doable, nothing too heavy. Give agni lot to work on at noon, yes! But give agni a lot to work on in the evening and, um, no bueno.

AGNI'S STRENGTH? IT DEPENDS.

You might be wondering, "What about my agni!? How is my agni? What IS my agni?" Your agni is just as unique as you are, so it depends.

Vatas have variable agni. Because of vata's unpredictability, they are irregular eaters with irregular agni. Sometimes they eat a lot and sometimes like a bird. Vatas are snacky eaters eating tiny meals all day and night. This irregularity causes them to be irregular with poop too — restarting digestion constantly causes bloating and constipation. If vatas are over hungry, they will get light headed, moody, weak and feel like they are going to pass out. Train agni to expect 3-4 square meals.

Pittas have strong agni. Overall pittas have the strongest agni because the fire element is most dominant in them. They can eat meat and tin cans and feel just fine. They are almost always hungry and can digest food really well. Because they are often so physically active, they tend to eat large quantities of food to keep them satisfied. But eating that way over a lifetime could make pittas gain weight. If pittas are not fed, they will get fierce! If they get fierce and you have no food handy, throw a piece of chocolate at them and run away.

Kaphas have weak agni. Kaphas have sluggish, cold qualities so their agni is low and consistent. They rarely say they are starving and if they are it's because they have not eaten in a day and a half. They can go a long time without eating and feel content in the mind and steady in body. Make no mistake though, kaphas love to eat! They love to experience and savor their food, but they don't need a lot of it. Kaphas have to be very mindful of building up toxins since they are the dosha that "builds." Kapha collects and that means food too, so their portions should be smaller because they are satisfied easier. If a kapha is not fed, it's fine, they can wait and still remain happy.

The bottom line is, we need to keep our agni burning strongly to digest our food or the old food turns into useless gobby toxins. Toxins clog channels, block channels, cause extra flow in the wrong channels, wrap themselves around the doshas (suffocating them) and might cause the doshas to flow in the wrong direction, going in places they shouldn't. When this happens we get sick. When toxins collect it's like old soggy food bits collecting in the kitchen sink drain. No bueno! Bad news! We have to melt them away and clean them out.

basic rules of agni

If you feel hunger
at the right time, eat.

Hunger is one of the best ways to determine if your agni is functioning properly.

Rule of thumb, if you are not hungry, don't eat. Fast and drink ginger tea to help agni catch up. When agni is ready for more food, we feel hunger.

Conversely if we don't eat when agni asks for food, agni gets weak and it shrinks. In this case when we do finally eat agni will be too small to digest food well.

If we skip breakfast when we are hungry, we don't give agni anything thing to grow on. Fire does not grow on a matchstick — it needs kindling. Matchsticks go out quickly.

Ama...toxins

Toxins are created by old food but not solely food. As with all things in Ayurveda, emotions, stressors, lifestyle and environment (all connected) also play a huge role in how we digest. Digestion is food, yes. But digestion also includes all information we absorb with the five senses, taste being only one of the five. When doshas are imbalanced due to lifestyle, diet, negative emotions, etc., agni's function becomes weakened or disturbed and leaves undigested food behind.

This undigested food turns into ama (AH-muh), which is a toxic, sticky, cloudy and smelly substance that can spread from the gastrointestinal tract to other parts of the body. From there it can lodge itself into crevices causing clogs in channels, blood vessels and cell membranes. Yum!

It sounds complicated and difficult to get ama, but it's kind of easy if we're not paying attention. How many times have we eaten on the go, while working, during an intense conversation, or while nervous? How many times have we gone back for seconds even though we were full? How often have we had an ice cold fizzy beverage with our meal? All of these eating practices can cause ama.

OH MAN, HOW DO WE GET AMA?

- Overeating
- Cold and goopy or raw foods (yogurt falls into this category)
- Eating before previous food is digested
- Eating when not hungry
- Ignoring indigestion (bloating, constipation, heartburn) and eating anyway
- Uncooked or undercooked food
- Sleeping after meals (wait 3 hours after eating before hitting the sack)
- Exercising after meals (wait at least 2 hours)
- Drinking a lot of water during or immediately after meals
- Ice cold drinks or carbonated drinks with meals
- Emotional unrest including; stress, anxiety, grief, fear, especially while eating
- Multitasking and eating

truth

Ever feel like your stomach is "burning" from hunger? That's a signal from agni! Honor that burn and give it some food.

more truth

Have you ever been so hungry that you are no longer hungry? That is when agni gets sad, gives up on you, and says, "forget it, I'm not getting food so I'm going to make myself smaller because I have no fuel or strength left."

still more truth

Clear burps are a sign your food has been fully digested. Don't eat if you are still burping your last meal. A wee bit grody, but the truth.

- Check your tongue — if it's got a white coating, that's ama
- Bad breath
- Energy level is low, sluggish, sleepy or weak
- Cloudy in the mind
- Feeling blockage in the body (constipation, congestion, joint pain)
- Not hungry or no taste for food/no appetite
- Tired or sluggish after meals
- Generally unmotivated and lethargic
- Unexplained aches, joint pains, and general malaise

You will be able to detect ama if you pay attention to these subtle signs. If you are feeling "off" in any way, check your tongue — ama shows up on our tongue. If your tongue is coated white, that's a sign you have ama (pausing while you all run to the mirror now…I know you).

Ama needs to be addressed before a person can fully heal.

Rather than being afraid of ama, let us thank it. It's not showing up because it's evil, it's showing up because we have some work to do on ourselves. This is a good way to think about it, "Thank you ama! I see you and understand that something is off balance. Thank you for bringing it to my attention. I'll get right on this. Now let's take a peek at my tongue…XO!"

Disclaimer: Putting an "XO" at the end of your little prayer to ama is optional which may or may not affect the results.

See "check your tongue!" over that-a-way

I ran and checked my tongue. OMG, I think I have ama!
First, don't freak out. Getting rid of ama can be simple or complex depending how long you've had the problem, and how deep in your tissues the ama is. Sometimes it takes an afternoon or skipping a meal to rid it or even months. Sometimes it takes a full Ayurvedic cleanse to remove it. Therefore, the treatment to clean out ama varies. It depends! If you have lots of ama and it's stubborn to get rid of, see an Ayurvedic practitioner for treatment.

---

you matter

If you are consistently sick and not finding results with your doctor, it might be worth exploring a panchakarma *(PAHN-cha-CAR-muh)* cleanse with a reputable Ayurvedic practitioner.

Panchakarma (p. 207) is an Ayurvedic cleanse that includes a mono diet and series of Ayurvedic therapies, which will last about three weeks. Imbalanced doshas are gathered from certain locations in the body and then expelled during the cleansing period. Ending with nourishing therapies, we rejuvenate and rebuild the body back to optimal health.

---

learn

If the tongue has a white coating which can be scraped off so the tongue turns pink, that is not ama. If the tongue has a white coating which cannot scrape off, that is ama.

check your tongue!

Our entire digestive system is reflected on the tongue. Every morning when you wake up, check your tongue. If you have a tongue scraper, scrape it a few times to get the night goo off it. After that, look again. If it is pink you are doing great! If it is white you may have ama.

Besides a white coating, there are other things we can look for on our tongue. If there is redness, it can indicate that there is too much heat in the body or that our digestion is too hot. If there are cracks on the tongue, that could mean dehydration or not enough healthy oils in the diet. If the tongue is shaky, that is a sign of anxiety, fear or too much movement. If there are little teeth marks on the side, it could be a sign of ama and/or unabsorbed nutrients in the colon.

cracked
dryness

dosha tongues

Vata. If vatas have a coating on their tongue, the root cause often comes from their dry and cold qualities — constipation or raw/cold foods that have not digested may show up as white on the tongue. Most common tongues for vata are cracked, shaky, or teeth marks on the edges. Too much movement (mind or body) and dryness causes those tongues. Vata tongues are skinny.

Pitta. Pittas likely have the pinkest tongues because they have strong digestion. If they run too hot their tongue will look red or cracked which is a clue that they need to cool down. If they run extra hot, their tongue may have a yellow coating, again, as a sign to cool down. Pitta tongues are pointy and sharp (literally and figuratively).

Kapha. Kaphas can easily collect a white coating because of their sticky nature. Skipping meals while sipping ginger tea will help as well as brothy soups with black pepper, garlic, and other pungent spices. It could take a full day, sometimes months, for the tongue to return to pink, depending how long the coating has been there. Kapha tongues are wide and round.

shaking
anxiety, worry, fear

white coating
sign of ama

HOW TO GET RID OF AMA

- Don't eat. Skip meals until you are hungry.
- Drink warm water (adding lime is good for vata) first thing in the morning
- Sip ginger tea (p. 145) or,
- Cumin, coriander and fennel tea ("CCF" tea p. 152)
- Eat light, warm, spicy, liquid foods like soups
- Use digesting spices like ginger and black pepper
- Do a mini at-home kitchari cleanse (p. 203)
- See an Ayurvedic practitioner for guidance

The best thing we can do when our tongue is white, drink hot water that has been boiled fresh and cooled enough to sip. We have to let our body catch up to the food we put in it and the only way it can do that is if we don't give it any more food. I don't mean a crazy fast for days. I mean sipping ginger (or herbal, but ginger is best because it increases digestive fire) tea for a few hours to let agni catch up. If you try it, I think you will find it fun to watch! When you are really hungry, I bet your tongue will be nice and pink. Try it!

HOW DO YOU KNOW WHEN YOU NO LONGER HAVE AMA?

- Your tongue is pink
- You have renewed energy
- You can wake up easily
- You are hungry for meals and don't feel heavy or tired after eating
- Your mind is clear and optimistic
- You are in a happy mood

There are no good or bad foods. Food is food. It depends on who is eating it, the state of their digestive fire, how they prepare it, how they eat it, and when they eat it.

ojas

What the heck is ojas?

Ojas *(OH-jus)* is the essential energy of our vitality, immunity, strength, luster and health. Ojas is the pure essence of all bodily tissues which means that after all the tissues in the body have gone through their transformative digestive processes, ojas is what is left. Ojas is our immunity and responsible for reproduction and creation. We only have a tiny bit, a few drops, and it lives in the heart. People with good ojas rarely get sick and often avoid even the most contagious office bugs. Conversely, those with low levels or low-quality ojas will get sick often.

When ojas is low, we feel physically and mentally weak, worried, anxious, unstable, and our complexion turns lifeless as our physical body gets rough and thin. When ojas is strong and healthy, the eyes are full of luster and life, we have confidence, clarity of mind, enhanced creativity, efficient digestion and potent fertility. Hooray! Love me some ojas! To produce enough high quality ojas, we need to put pure nourishment in our bodies.

What enhances ojas?

- Ghee is the best ojas enhancer
- Organic whole milk (raw milk is primo if you can find it)
- Good quality sleep
- Proper diet according to your doshas with foods close to nature
- Stress management through various pranayama (p. 165) including; *nadi shodhanam, kapalabhati,* and/or *so hum.*

What depletes ojas?

- Improper diet including: excessive alcohol, caffeine, carbonated drinks, fast food, stale food, reheated, microwaved, frozen, overly cold or raw foods
- Anything in excess including work, stress, worry/anxiety, sex and exercise
- Lack of sleep or poor quality sleep
- Overall sadness, consistent irritability or anger

● ● ● ● ● ● ● ● ●

ojas facts

Ojas is pronounced *OH-jus.* Not *OH-has.* It's Sanskrit, not Spanish.

After sex, have a small glass of milk to replenish ojas.

Lifeless, canned, processed foods have no life, no prana and will not build ojas.

When you have enough ojas, the mind will be content.

Ojas increases with heavy foods, but if you can't digest it, it turns to ama.

● ● ● ● ● ● ● ● ●

What about poop?

truth

In case nobody ever mentioned it, you should poop every day. The only way we can tell what's happening on the insides is by what comes out. If you don't poop everyday, you are constipated and that is something to work on.

philosophy

Constipation can cause headaches. Think of it as a traffic jam of poop. The poo is all jammed in our digestive tract which eventually affects the highways (channels) all the way up to our head. Headaches are said to be a call from God because they are such a painful nuisance (sometimes debilitating), we can't help but notice and make change.

YAY FOR POOP

Ayurveda talks a lot about poop. Why? Because it is a direct reflection of our digestion, which is of #1 importance. If poop doesn't come out, that means we are keeping the garbage inside. If we poop too much, we might not be absorbing the nutrients from the food like we should. Look at your poop! It's important.

Now that I've broken the ice, let's go into poop mode a little more.

Ideal poop. Ideally, you should go in the morning after waking up. If you are really healthy, your need to go might even wake you up. That's awesome. The poop should be one solid piece — like a big brown banana (oh, come on, you can handle it). It may or may not float. However! If there are any fats/oils in your poop or floating on the water, that is not good. That means there is so much fat/oil in the body that is not getting digested properly. According to the classic Ayurvedic texts, the perfect poop actually makes a special splash noise that goes, "ding!" Um. If you poop a "ding!" I would really love to know about it and I will send you some kind of prize.

Sinking poop. If your poop sinks, it could mean you ate something that's too heavy or off harmony with your natural balance. It could also be a sign of toxins, but that's not always true either. You can correct sinking poop mostly by changing your diet and eating foods that balance your dosha(s). For example, a pitta person might eat salads and their poop will float. A vata person might eat salads and their poop will sink. It's per your individual balance.

Seeing food in the poop. This could mean that your food is not being digested or absorbed. Certain foods just don't get broken down and others may not have been cooked properly. So it goes in and comes right out. A main cause is not chewing the food properly. Our stomach says, "I dunno what to do with this…I don't have teeth. I'll just send to the intestines and colon and let them deal with it." And out it goes.

Constipation. Constipation is a vata problem because of the dry and light qualities. The colon is the seat of vata and a good clue that someone has increased vata vikruti is that they can't poop. It's mostly due to dryness where the little stoolies get all hard and can't move. A person may not be eating enough oils/fats (lubrication) and/or not drinking enough water. Constipation has a major effect on concentration, moods and can cause headaches. Literally the crap stays inside and it toxifies the enitre system. Unreleased emotions can also cause constipation. For the sake of pooping, learn to let it go.

Diarrhea. According to Ayurveda, if someone has diarrhea, let them have it! The body is trying to rid something, so let it work itself out. The problem occurs when it turns to pure water and then it needs to be stopped. For the most part though, the body is angry about what's inside and it needs to get rid of it. As long as it's not frequent, just let it happen. If it's frequent, a nutritional (and maybe emotional) check is in order.

Loose poop in pieces. Pitta types usually experience poop in pieces. And they tend to poop more than once a day. Their fire and water elements cause the poop to lose its form a little and can be too watery. Healthy amounts of fiber would help dry it out a little so it sticks together in a nice poo form. Sometimes vatas feel like the poop wasn't complete — like they still have to go. That could be because the pieces are breaking off and not coming out all the way.

Big, lots o' poop. Kaphas will have a very healthy poop (probably why they are always so happy) and there will be a lot of it. Kaphas have to look for any excess oil or mucus in their stools. If there is, it means that there is too much heaviness in the body and is a sign of ama. Kaphas need to keep up with their fiber and veggies to get their poop to float.

Really smelly poop. I don't know any poop that smells like roses but if it really stinks, that's not a good sign. It's a sign of ama and/or a sign that the food didn't get absorbed all the way. Perhaps the body could not process what was eaten.

just for you

The poop section was not even going to make it into this book but I had several people ask me if I was going to include a chapter on poop. No, not a chapter. But here's your poop scoop.

resource

A funny and informative little book: *What's Your Poo Telling You?,* by Josh Richman and Anish Sheth, MD

7

NEW-TRITION

You are what you digest

ayur-tip

In Ayurveda, HOW you eat
is just as important
as what you eat.

truth

Pay attention to the foods you
eat. Food is food but provides a
certain action on the body.
Whether your individual body
will benefit from that action,
is how you know which foods
will balance you the most.

AYURVEDIC VS. WESTIE NUTRITION

Ayurveda sees eating as a ritual that not only nourishes the body, but nourishes the mind and soul, too. According to experienced practitioners, it is said that most disease comes from wrong diet and wrong habits. In Ayurveda, food is our medicine which means that if we eat correctly, we won't need medicine. Food provides the building blocks to nourish and replenish our tissues, which make up our entire physical foundation and feeds the mind.

Ayurveda sees eating as a practice that not only nourishes the body, but nourishes the mind and soul, too.

Managing our lifestyle and diet are essential components to treat imbalanced doshas and the key to disease prevention. Just like the rest of Ayurveda, diet and nutrition are uniquely dependent on your dosha. As a bonus, you might be happy to hear that calories, scales and food pyramid do not exist in Ayurveda! Freedom! Instead, we focus on when to eat, how to eat, how we feel after eating and balancing the six tastes (p. 124). Ayurveda also emphasizes the importance of eating with peace and happiness (not stressed or while multi-tasking).

Contrary to what might people might think, eating "Ayurvedically" is not complex or restrictive. It's actually freeing once you know what foods are best for your dosha — nutrition customization just for you! Foods have qualities and actions on the body and mind! Remember our friends, "the qualities?" Yep, they are in foods, too. By learning the types of foods that jibe best with your dosha, and listening to what you really need, you will be spot on with your nutrition, honoring your unique diet for yourself. You will know how much food is too much and too little based on how you feel. You will also know when to honor cravings and when not to.

Distinct differences between our Western view of nutrition and the Ayurvedic viewpoint are in the chart on page 106. You can see they don't relate to each other much at all. If this is your first experiencing delving into any eastern science, shifting to understand nutrition this way might feel a little foreign. But keep an open mind as you let it sink in a little bit, even if not counting calories totally blows your mind.

WHEN DIET IS
WRONG
MEDICINE IS OF NO USE

WHEN DIET IS
CORRECT
MEDICINE IS OF NO NEED

Why do we eat: Westie. Westies (that's what I like to call us Westerners) tend to totally complicate our food to the point where the idea of eating is no longer enjoyable and doesn't have much to do with actual food. Am I wrong? We might eat foods based on what we think are "good foods" while avoiding "bad foods." Or, we might make choices based on what tastes overly good, ignoring the ingredients in the food. We may live on one side of the pendulum either hyper-aware or completely ignorant to the ingredients in the food.

Westies might eat out of habit — ever get stuck in that rut? Cheese sandwiches galore before realizing you have not had a vegetable in a month?

Westies might also eat for social reasons based on what the group is having or on what someone else is having. "Even though I'm full, if you are having a sundae for dessert, I'll have one too." Or maybe you are at a dinner party, chatting away, not realizing that you have just eaten a dozen of the crab puffed appetizers. Whoops.

Physical appearance is probably the biggest driver of the Westies' nutritional decisions. Fad diets have been around forever. And we buy it. We buy the books, the recipes, do what the celebrities do, purchase the online subscriptions and fad diets…and they don't work. Then we feel a big fail, so we try another one. Rinse and repeat.

	WESTIE NUTRITION	AYURVEDIC NUTRITION
Why do we eat?	Food preference, habit, social, physical appearance, emotions	Take in prana (life) and build the physical body
Food focus	Calories and counting them	How our individual body processes what we eat
Food balance	The five food groups	Balancing the six tastes
Philosophy	"You are what you eat"	"You are what you digest"

Westies may also eat food to fill emotional voids. Sometimes we eat out of happiness (big feast!) and sometimes out of loneliness (hand me the ice cream spoon). We eat out of stress and we eat in a rush because we are too busy to sit down and take time for a meal. Our emotions drive our decision to eat rather than physical hunger so we need to strike a balance to gently nourish our emotional body without giving extra food to our physical bodies.

Why do we eat: Ayurvedic. We eat to take in prana. Prana is life energy given to us by the purity of nature, the nourishment of food and our breath. If we do not have prana, we will not function properly. We eat to nourish our tissues and build our body of good things. We eat to nourish our mind so we can make good decisions and adhere to right action. We eat for energy. We eat because we are hungry. We eat to live. We eat with thanks. We eat with love.

Prana is life energy given to us by the purity of nature, the nourishment of food and our breath.

Food focus: Westie. A Westie diet measures how many calories we consume based on our gender and how active we are. It's a number that "counts" food, basically. Food is weighed and numbered and so are we. Um, how are we supposed to enjoy food if we are so busy counting it?!

Food focus: Ayurvedic. Ayurveda does not measure food in calories. That's right — no calories in Ayurveda! I swear it's true. Freedom from calories! For those pittas raising an eyebrow, stay with me. As we move through how foods are digested from an Ayurvedic viewpoint, it will make more sense.

I have a calories story: In 2007, I was a personal trainer in San Francisco and was seeing a Westie nutritionist. I wanted to know what I should be eating for ME (I had not yet discovered Ayurveda). And here's what I got: Because I was "burning extra calories" by standing around teaching a fitness class, I should eat five or six meals a day totaling around 2,000 calories. I am 5' 4," by the way. The plan didn't really resonate with me, but I tried it. I was eating ALL the time. I felt constantly full. I was and bloated and could not poop. I was totally plugged up from my head to my toenails with food. I gained, probably 8 lbs in a few weeks (just a guess 'cause I've never owned a scale). Overall, I felt sluggish and heavy and sad.

truth

Try holding your breath. How long before you die? Mmkay. Prana is the most important thing we need to live. We will die without prana.

About a month later, I began Ayurveda school and once I learned Ayurvedic nutrition, I never went back to calor-oonies. To this day, I don't even think about them and instead just listen to my body. No need to count, just bring awareness to eating and you'll get there, too.

Food balance: Westie. Westies balance the five food groups which are: meat, dairy, grains, fruits and vegetables. It is said we all need certain amounts of each one of these groups daily to stay balanced.

Food balance: Ayurvedic. The problem Ayurveda has with the food pyramid is not all people are the same, so their foods should not be all the same either. There are a few things Ayurveda does to balance foods which can get complicated, so for easy digestibility I'll break it down into easy pieces.

Instead of calories, Ayurveda focuses on the six tastes. The six tastes are: sweet, salty, sour, pungent, bitter and astringent. Each one of those tastes has specific qualities, like cold, light, hot, sharp, heavy, etc., just like the doshas do. We will talk in depth about the tastes in chapter 8.

Philosophy: Westie. "You are what you eat" is what the Westies say. And that's not wrong. If you eat crappy things, you will feel and look like crap. However what this leaves out is the quality of digestion *after* you eat certain foods.

Philosophy: Ayurvedic. Remember back in chapter 2, when we talked about the ground rules? Let's revisit the Ayurvedic philosophy, "you are what you digest."

No matter how "healthy" the food is, if we cannot digest it, it is not going to be absorbed and used as fuel. The food will either get stuck somewhere inside, or it will go out the other end. For example, if eating spicy sausages gives us the poops in 30 minutes, we are not digesting that food well — it's just going out the back door. So, our body gives us a hint, "Hey! I'm quickly pooping out all this sausage 'cause I can't digest it!" Or, if we are eating lots of raw vegetables and have not pooped in four days, we are not digesting that food well either — it's all stuck inside.

Get it? If we don't digest our food, we cannot use it. If we cannot use it, we don't get prana. If we don't get high quality ojas and prana, we will get sick. When we digest foods properly, food is fuel and the fuel has to make it through our system so that it can be used and assimilated. The unused stuff turns into poop and out it goes.

How we eat: Ayurvedic only. Westie nutrition does not address HOW we eat. And I don't mean using a fork in the right or left hand. I mean, because mind, body and spirit are connected, we need to eat with a peaceful and happy mind. Like, not eating when we are stressed is super important! It is safe to say that eating on the go, in a car, while upset or at our desk at work are not health-promoting ways to eat, even if the food is totally perfect and balancing for us!

One of my teachers told us this little story: If we are starving to the point of getting light-headed (vata) or getting angry (pitta), we would do more damage to stop at the store to get fixin's for a perfectly organic dinner, go home, make the dinner and eat it. With the hour(s) that passes, our digestive fire (agni) will be really low and our mind will be out of sorts. This is not honoring our hunger. She said we are better off to pick up something to-go and sit in a park and eat it with a happy mind, enjoying our surroundings. In this example, honoring our hunger and eating with peace of mind will do our bodies more good than struggling to buy the very best food. Does that mean blissfully eat a bag of Oreos? No, dude. It means do the best you can with the tools you have, without wrecking your mind, mood or body to achieve perfection.

We've got to warm our food with our spirit or our body will not accept it.

If we are stressed, rushed, worried, depressed, sad, lonely, etc., putting food into our body is one of the worst things we can do because the body will be busy tending to our emotions in need. When the body is tending to emotions, it is not focused on digestion, agni is not strong, and our food remains undigested. We've got to warm our food with our spirit or our body will not accept it. Everything in our body rises to welcome the food.

food

Fiber is light and airy. Pittas and kaphas will do just fine with fiber and in fact, kaphas need it. Vatas will cry with too much fiber. There is too much air, space and fluffiness in it, which will cause poor vatas bellies to bloat and cramp. So sad.

you matter

If any food makes you feel bad in some way, stop eating it. Your body is telling you you cannot digest it well and it is not the best choice for you.

What should the doshas eat?

Vata (space & air). Our vata friends are cold, dry, rough, light, and mobile. So the foods they eat need to be opposite of that which means warm, moist, smooth, heavy and grounding.

Because vatas have wind and space in them, some of their biggest digestive complaints are gas, bloating and constipation. They are so light in body that if food isn't heavy enough it stays in their digestive tract, like little hot air balloons. Vatas need foods that are heavy enough to ground their mind, build and nourish their body, and pull the food down and out! That's why vatas need a good amount of oils and water/moisture in their food. Moist and heavy foods will move downward so that vata can digest them nicely. If a vata eats popcorn and pretzels all the time, those foods (dry and light) will just stay dry and light in their guts too and not to mention, they won't ever be satisfied.

Despite vatas wanting to eat healthy and light, vatas cannot digest salads or raw veggies well. They will instantly feel bloated and wonder why because they are "eating so healthy." They will be far better off having a bowl of rice with ghee or oatmeal with almond butter.

To stay satiated and balanced, vatas should eat three to four square meals. Vatas tend to graze all day, like munchy little goats. Nibble nibble nibble for hours. Constant snacking increases the movement quality in their digestion because it will be constantly working and therefore will increase vata energy (movement increases movement). Increasing vata will make them more munchy, more gassy, more bloatey.

foodie

It is not uncommon for vatas to go crazy with the salads. Vatas will likely be the dosha most vocal and fearful about gaining weight and watching what they eat. The irony is that it is naturally hard for them to gain weight. So what happens is they give their bodies a rough go with too many salads and end up constipated, moody, constantly snacking, under weight and usually sick.

LIFE CHECK   WHAT TO EAT? VATA FOODS

What are foods that have warm, sticky, saucy, grounding qualities?
Hint: Think "comfort" foods. List:

_____
_____
_____
_____
_____
_____
_____
_____

Pitta (fire & water). Our pitta friends are hot, sharp, slightly oily, smooth, light, mobile. So pittas need to favor cooling, mild, less oily, grounding, calming foods.

Pittas tend to run hot because they have the fire element in them, so they have an advantage to digesting food really well. Because their fire is so strong, they have the opposite problem of a vata or kapha and sometimes can digest too quickly and too hotly. Because of that, pittas should have warm foods, but not super spicy or acidic foods because extra "heat" could hyper-increase agni. Pittas should favor protein, fresh fruits and veggies with healthy and clean carbs — a pretty well rounded plate. Fruits and veggies provide a sweet coolness that soothes pittas, while carbs will satisfy their intense hunger. Pittas also need to add protein whether from plants or animals — they are the dosha that digests meat the best. The best choice of meat for pitta is fish. Red meat is more heating than fish or chicken, which is why some pittas tend to get heartburn after their big steak dinner.

Pittas should also eat three square meals a day, but might need a snack in the morning around 10 a.m. and possibly also around 3 p.m. The danger for pittas is that their agni gets increased to a level that might be too high, causing them to overeat which can cause weight gain. Just because their fire is very strong, doesn't mean that they need lots of extra food. Choosing the right foods will be most important. Pittas will chug cool water, like, all day long. Their heat burns off water through sweat and pee and just from working so hard, so they tend to be thirsty to replenish their water supply.

LIFE CHECK WHAT TO EAT? PITTA FOODS

What are foods that have cooling, mild, grounding, calming qualities?
Hint: Think "fresh" foods. List:

_____

_____

_____

_____

_____

_____

_____

_____

I'm two doshas! What do I eat?

When our prakruti is two doshas, we will find that the qualities are mostly opposites. In that case, eat in harmony with the seasons and pay attention to how we feel when we eat certain foods. There is also likely to be a common thread between the dosha qualities (Are both warm? Are both cool?) so we can balance that quality consistently.

Balancing nutrition with the seasons means that a pitta in summer will always choose cooling foods while avoiding spicy, meaty dishes with a carafe of red wine. A kapha in spring will always choose light, dry, warm foods avoiding fettuccine alfredo. A vata in fall or winter will choose grounding, warm foods and avoid a crispy salad with ice cream for dessert.

It's a little trial and error, but here's the thing: If we screw up we'll feel a little like junk. Great! You learned. Chalk the foodie experiments as part of the journey to getting to know yourself and then begin adhering to the choices that make you feel awesome. Before you know it, you'll be an expert at *your* nutrition.

Kapha (water & earth). Our kapha friends are cold, wet, heavy and static. They need foods that are warm, dry, light and well-spiced to stay balanced.

Kaphas are naturally steady and heavy, with low and consistent agni. Their diet should be largely vegetarian and should favor warm veggie dishes with light, warm grains like quinoa, basmati rice or barley. They can also enjoy high-fiber fruits, like apples or pears, but should avoid large amounts of very sweet and heavy fruits like bananas, coconuts and avocados. Kaphas are oily, so the foods they choose should be more dry. Otherwise, kapha will feel heavy and sloshy.

Most of all, pay attention to how you FEEL after you eat.

Kaphas don't need to eat a lot of food. Ayurveda recommends kaphas skip dinner at least once a week. This gives their agni a chance to catch up and digest any old food stuffs. Some of the worst things a kapha can do is eat a cold, wet breakfast and eat a late dinner because these habits work against their agni. Their agni is not strong enough for either of these as a habit and over time will definitely cause a kapha imbalance.

LIFE CHECK   WHAT TO EAT? KAPHA FOODS

What are foods that have warm, dry, light qualities?
Hint: Think "light and spicy" foods. List:

_____

_____

_____

_____

_____

Eating is going to become such a fresh journey for you now. Your awareness will expand as you start paying attention to how the foods feel in your body. You are going to awaken to a whole new way of eating once you have been given permission to let go of what everyone else says you "should" be eating and instead, just eat what makes you feel best.

As you transition, the process may feel little ambiguous but try not to over think it because every body truly is different. Without calories or portion control as a guide, it might be a little tough to know "what is right for me." But if you eat three times per day and have a snack when your body calls for it, that is a good start. You are the best gauge on how foods make you feel. Just start paying attention.

Every body is different.
But you knew that...

By now you know that every body and every agni is you-nique! Vatas have varied digestion, kaphas have slow by steady digestion and pittas have strong digestion. Not all foods are good for all people, even if they are organic, fair trade and in season. It's important to make sure the foods you eat balance the qualities of your doshas.

LET'S EXPLORE A LESSON IN USING THE BEST INGREDIENTS TO MAKE YOU-NIQUE MEALS.

Too cold for vata. Let's take some baby spinach, arugula, radishes, green onion, carrots, shredded brussels sprouts, broccoli and cauliflower. Toss it all together and create a big salad! Veggielicious. With all these delicious organic veggies straight from the farmers market - how could it not be good? Now, invite your vata friend over for lunch. She's thin, gets chilly easily, talks a heck of a lot, and bundles in layers with fuzzy socks even when it's warm outside. She is always quite vocal in her complaints about her digestive problems including frequent bloating and gassiness, so she likes to eat as healthy as possible. Plus, she does NOT want to gain weight! You thought this would be the perfect meal because there's nothing healthier than all these veggies!

For a vata however, this salad would be one of the worst things they can eat. Vata is already cold, dry, light and adding these cold, dry, light foods will make her uncomfortable and bloated in 30 minutes or less. This salad is totally raw so the element of fire has not been introduced, which makes agni's job much harder. Vatas already have weak or variable agni, so this food will sit in vata's guts and cause trouble. (Bloat-bloat. Puff-puff. Cramp.)

Let's do another one.

Too hot for pitta. Pretend it's summer and you pick up some tomatoes, red peppers and fresh garlic at the farmers market. Tomatoes, peppers and garlic are heating foods. Your witty, smart pitta friend, who has red hair, freckles, bright blue eyes and fair pinkish skin is coming over for dinner. Using your tomatoes, peppers and garlic, you serve her a lovely bowl of gazpacho and bread served up with some red sangria. And what better place to eat than on your back deck in the hot sunshine!

After eating and chatting, you soon notice your pitta friend has blotchy red skin on her neck and chest. Her freckles are multiplying and you notice her

water rules

water bubbles

Avoid carbonated beverages at least on a regular basis. The tiny bubbles are full of air, which float up. We want our squishy warm bodies to maintain downward flow and the bubbles create reversal. If you feel like you are going to hiccup when taking a sip of soda, that is a perfect example of the upward-airy movement of the bubbles. The body is signaling that it's not doing down right.

water facts

Did you know 2/3 of the Earth is water? Did you know that 2/3 of our bodies is water, too? YES! Three cheers! Drink up so we don't cause a drought within.

Bones have only 31% water in them. Bones are vata in physical form because the bones have tons of little holes (air and space!) in them. Compared to the rest of the body, bones are…bone dry.

"Drink eight glasses of water per day."

"For weight loss, drink a glass of water before meals because you won't eat as much."

"Divide your body weight by half, change that to ounces, and that's how much water you should drink per day."

I'm sure you've heard or read some of these statements about drinking water. Because you know some good things about Ayurveda now, you are learning to ask your body first before adhering to diet or nutrition statements you read or hear from the outside. Let's deepen your knowledge and see how much water each dosha might need.

Vatas are bone dry. Because of their dry quality and lack of water element, vatas need a moderate amount of water, but tend not to drink enough (they forget, poor things). It is very important for vatas to stay hydrated and well-oiled so they have nice poops and therefore nice moods and positive thoughts. If they are too dry, they will be constipated and so sad. Note: If vatas have *too* much water it can cause indigestion.

Pittas are hot. Pittas need the most water. They are thirstier because of their fire element which creates heat which evaporates sweat and requires them to replenish often. Pittas diligently remember to drink their water and they will crave it, too.

Kapha are full o' water. Kaphas naturally have lots of water in them so they don't need as much water as the other two doshas. Kaphas also have low agni, so too much water will squelch the fire they do have going. Bonus: Kaphas are slow to wrinkle because of all that water!

skin is looking pretty red even though you have only been outside for 20 minutes. She might experience some heartburn, but she probably won't mention it.

Even though the foods are fresh and organic, the qualities of the tomatoes, peppers, garlic and alcohol are all hot. And way too hot for this Irish pitta gal who now has a little inferno in her body!

Let's do one more for kapha.

Too cold 'n' gooey for kapha. Your kapha friend is coming over for breakfast before you two enjoy a day of shopping. You know that she doesn't eat breakfast because she's not usually hungry early in the morning. But to be hospitable (because she always is), you whip up an easy yogurt parfait! You have fresh berries and some full-fat Greek yogurt (because Monica B told you not to eat low-fat anything), and granola, all from the farmers market. You decide to layer the goods in a glass — first the granola on the bottom, then berry mixture, then a dollop of yogurt, and repeat twice! It's a glorious striped beauty of health! Your kapha friend is sure to smile with joy at your pretty creation.

So. This breakfast is not good for anyone, but kaphas in particular will have a very hard time with it. Yogurt increases kapha, berries are sour which increases kapha, and granola is too oily, nutty and heavy for kapha. The parfait is also cold, which dampens or extinguishes kapha's already weak agni. AND! Fruit and dairy are considered incompatible foods (p. 156) in Ayurveda. Meaning, when they mix in our belly they actually fight with swords (that might be an exaggeration) while going down, instead of holding hands, smiling and going down the slide together.

Take a broad view and have variety. So again, just because the foods are organic and natural, doesn't mean they suit all people all of the time. Absolutely not the case. If you are a pitta and eat a tomato or pepper, it will not kill you but you might notice problems if you have them regularly. Overall, have less of those foods. Zoom out and take a broader view of your diet favoring the foods that balance you best and eating less of those that don't.

VATA = COLD, DRY, LIGHT. SALADS ARE NO BUENO.

PITTA = HOT, SHARP. SPICY FOODS ARE NO BUENO.

KAPHA = COLD, HEAVY, WET. YOGURT IS NO BUENO.

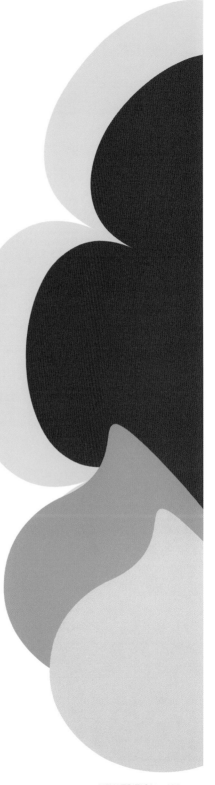

nutritional guidelines

EAT ACCORDING TO YOUR DOSHA

SMALL BREAKFAST, BIG LUNCH,
SMALL DINNER

EAT WHAT IS IN SEASON

**AVOID STALE, CANNED AND/OR
PROCESSED FOODS**

AVOID ICE WATER

LEAVE SPACE

EAT WHEN HUNGRY, AT THE RIGHT TIME

CLEAR BURPS

CHEW WELL

FOCUS ON THE FOOD

DON'T MULTITASK AND EAT

FEED SOMEONE ELSE
BEFORE FEEDING YOURSELF

EAT IN A HAPPY MOOD

BLESS AND THANK YOUR FOOD

AYURVEDIC NUTRITIONAL GUIDELINES

Eat according to your dosha. Pretty sure we get this by now. A customized approach to eating is exactly what we need to stay balanced. If you are heavy, eat light. If you are cold, eat warm. If you are light, eat heavy. If you are hot, avoid spicy. And so on. Eating meals that balance your unique combination is crucial.

Small breakfast, big lunch, small dinner. Remembering the story of agni, we should eat according to where the sun is. Have a small breakfast to kindle agni, large lunch to satiate agni and a small dinner as agni winds down. Remember, when the sun sets our heart closes like a little flower and the entire body slows down.

Eat what is in season. Seasonal vegetables and fruits come straight from the rain, the soil and the sun. They pop up just at the right time of year to effortlessly bloom and ripen, perfectly in season. Because nature is smarter than we are (don't take it personally), we should favor foods in season rather than out-of-season. Eating watermelon in Wisconsin on Christmas is an example of out-of-season food and not the greatest choice.

In addition to seasonal balance, eating foods that are close to the source (earth/mud, water/rain, fire/sun) are easier for us to digest and process. By eating foods that are close to the source of nature (i.e. not bologna or Velveeta), you will take in more prana (life energy) because they come directly from the five elements.

Avoid stale, canned and/or processed foods. Stale foods are past their prime, so toss them. There is no prana in that food and your body deserves way better. Canned foods have had the life sucked out of them so they can last a long time. Any food that can last a long time is a good indication that the food is very low in prana. Processed foods are along the same lines. These foods may have been created from nature, but they have been modified by man-made chemicals. A good rule of thumb is if you cannot pronounce and identify the ingredients on the label, don't buy or eat it. Lifeless foods equals lifeless nutrition equals lifeless us!

> **Good rule of thumb is, if you cannot pronounce and identify the ingredients on the label, don't buy or eat it.**

Avoid ice or very cold water, especially with meals. Cold water weakens or extinguishes agni. And what is our goal? Yep, to build and keep agni strong! Plus our bodies are warm and squishy, so anything too frigid will be a shock to the system. That shock *brrr* makes channels constrict, reduces flow and cools agni.

challenge

Fast foods are processed foods and carry zero prana. If you are eating a lot of fast foods or soft drinks, try to stop for one month. You may go back to the fast foods and sodas only to realize they don't taste good and you don't even miss them.

Avoid drinking a bunch of water before or after meals. Sipping a glass of water with your meal is perfect. Putting in too much water at meal time will dampen our agni just when we need it the most. Our bodies need the right measure of food and water to mix well. Not enough water and it won't be liquefied enough to digest — kind of like an overstuffed washing machine with soap but no water.

Leave space. Us Westies tend to eat until we are full. In Ayurveda if we eat until we are full, we have over-eaten. Let's go back to that washing machine. If we fill the washing machine all the way up with clothes and stuff it shut, where will the water go? How will it jiggle to get the clothes clean? How will sudsing happen? It won't! The washing machine will be overfull and proper agitation won't happen. Clothes can't get clean or rinsed and everything stays in a mucky white scummy wet blob that goes nowheres (OK, maybe that was just in the '80s when detergent left white scum). Same with our food. No mucky!

> ### If we eat until we feel full, we have already over-eaten.

Ayurveda says, fill the stomach three-quarters full. Half with food and one quarter with liquid. Leave one quarter as space so the food can mix and digest. For happy laundry, do this with your washing machine, too.

Eat only when you have real hunger and at the right time. As you know, us Westies eat for a variety of reasons and some of them have nothing to do with physical hunger. If you are not hungry, it's not only OK, but sometimes necessary to a skip meal.

Clear burps. Ha! This was one of my most favorite "T.M.I." statements that I learned in school. Foody burps are a sign your body is not done digesting. Sounds grody, but if you are still burping up your last meal, don't eat again until your burps are clear.

Chew well. Digestion starts in our mouth, did you know that? Saliva is kapha rushing in to start the juicy digestive process. Since chewing is the very first stage of digestion, bring a mindfulness to it. Teeth and saliva break down food and send it on its merry way to the stomach. In case you didn't know, the stomach doesn't have teeth. So whatever the teeth don't break down gets tossed down the hatch and either gets pushed aside, creates a clog, gives us indigestion or is sent out the other end. If you want to know how many times to chew, 32 is the magic number. Try it in your next meal and I bet you will taste many more flavors, you will slow down and you won't get a tummy ache!

Focus on the food. Our meal should have our undivided attention while we chew, taste and appreciate our food. Westies mindlessly munch and snack, often as a daily habit. We walk around the office with snacks in hand, grab a cookie near the printer and eat at our desk. We might come home and run straight to the cupboard to grab something before dinner because we are starving (I'm guilty!) and before we know it, we have NO idea how much food we have put in our bodies. Putting our mind in our eating habits will help us realize real hunger and real fullness and give us a new appreciation for eating as a ritual, not just as something else to check off our list of things to do.

Don't multitask and eat. We will confuse the heck out of our body if we are trying to do a few other things and gulp down food at the same time. The mind will be doing one thing and the body will be trying to digest what you are eating. But the body will not digest well without the mind telling it what to do. As soon as we start doing something else with our body, our mindful leaves the digestive system to finish accomplishing whatever else you are working on. The result is (you guessed it), old food hanging out, undigested.

Feed someone else before feeding yourself. Serve your friends and family first, even if it's your dog. There is generosity, grace and sharing involved in eating, so as a practice make sure everyone at the table is content and has what they need before feeding yourself.

Eat in a happy mood. Eat in a happy mood with a peaceful mind. If we are stressed, upset, angry, sad, etc., our body will be focused on trying to nurture our mood and the food won't get digested properly. And then we will have a tummy ache and some ama to go along with our already bummed out feelings.

Bless and thank your food. Gratitude is the quickest way to a healthy mind. Give your food a sincere blessing of thanks for the nourishment.

LIFE CHECK YOUR NUTRITION GUIDELINES

Which guidelines do you already practice?

Which guidelines would you like to start incorporating?

Are there any that would be hard for you to incorporate?
What are some ideas you have to overcome the obstacle?

YOU ARE WHAT YOU DIGEST

8
TASTE-BUDS

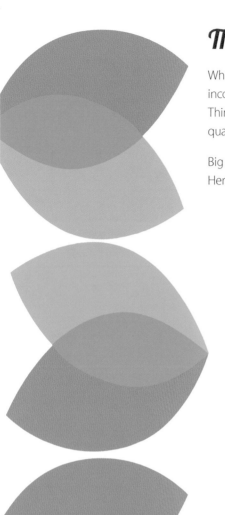

The six tastes

While we should favor foods that balance our qualities, we also need to incorporate a variety of tastes into every meal. There are six tastes in Ayurveda. Think of them as umbrellas over foods. Each is made of its own elements and qualities; therefore the foods that fall under that taste have similar qualities.

Big surprise, the six tastes are made up of the five great elements! Here's how they shake out:

SWEET
{earth & water}

SOUR
{earth & fire}

SALTY
{water & fire}

PUNGENT
{fire & air}

BITTER
{air & space}

ASTRINGENT
{air & earth}

Remembering like increases like, if we either omit or over indulge in any one of the tastes, there will be imbalance due to a lack of, or excess of elements. Certain tastes are more balancing for vata, pitta and kapha. Ayurveda says we should have all six tastes in each meal for proper digestion and to satisfy the mind. When we do this, our tissues will be built, toned and perfectly nourished, while keeping agni strong and our mind calm and sharp.

Incorporating every taste into each meal can sound a little daunting, but with a plate of veggies, fruits, carbs and protein and some spices, it's easy to incorporate all of them.

> **If we eat meals that contain all six tastes, our tissues will be built, toned and perfectly nourished, while keeping agni strong and our mind calm and sharp.**

SWEET

Sweet taste balances vata and pitta, while it increases kapha. Sweet is not limited to sugar but includes: all complex carbohydrates, milk, sweet fruits, root vegetables, oils, nuts, honey and meats. Refined or lab-made "sugars" are false tastes and therefore no bueno because they interfere with normal metabolic pathways.

Sweet in balance. Sweet taste is heavy, oily and cooling, a wholesome builder for the body, giving structure, grounding, nourishment and rejuvenation. These foods build ojas and create health when used properly. Sweet is the reason the body grows, it improves circulation and relieves heartburn! Sweet promotes stability in the body and in turn keeps the mind calm and happy, too.

Sweet in excess. Too much sweet will over-build us, which can cause congestion, heaviness, laziness, obesity and diabetes. It will also create heaviness in the mind which includes greed, envy and possessiveness.

SOUR

Sour taste is balancing for vata and increases pitta and kapha. Examples of the sour taste include: unsweetened yogurt, citrus fruits, most fresh fruit juices, alcohol, pickles, vinegary or fermented foods, "sour" cheeses and Sour Patch Kids® (just seeing if you were paying attention). Sour taste is heating, which helps stoke agni, improves appetite, promotes heat internally and cold externally and moistens the tissues. Sour is slightly oily, penetrating (sharp) and a good laxative. It destroys semen, constipation (obstruction), flatulence and vision.

---

nourish

Balancing the six tastes reduces cravings and helps us maintain ideal weight (whether gain or loss is needed). Our Westie diet generally consists mostly of sweet, salty and sour tastes. Unless we pay attention, it is easy to miss out on the pungent, bitter and astringent tastes. This is one of the causes of overeating and/or emotional eating for so many people. The power in the tastes lies in their variety and balance because each taste has a specific action on the body and mind. Variety rounds out the benefits of each taste that we all need.

Each taste has a compliment that balances them:
Sweet – Pungent
Sour – Astringent
Salt – Bitter

Sour in balance. Sour taste is heating so it improves digestion, reduces gas, increases circulation, liquefies mucus (but if it's not expelled, it clogs the channels) and sharpens the senses. Sour provides a refreshing palate cleanse therefore stimulating our appetite and stoking agni.

Sour in excess. Too much of the sour taste can cause heating problems like heartburn, acid reflux and ulcers. Too much heat and acidity result in burning sensations in the chest and inflamed skin problems like acne or eczema, blindness, itching and herpes to name a few.

It is salt's job to compel us to take in more nutrients by making food tasty.

SALTY

Salty taste is balancing for vata, while it increases pitta and kapha. There are a variety of salts like sea, Himalayan (the best!), table (no bueno), rock salt, even kelp! It is salt's job to compel us to take in more nutrients by making food tasty and it helps utilize what has been taken in. Salt is heating and retains water, which greatly benefits vata. Pittas do not need extra heat and kaphas do not need extra water.

Salt in balance. Salt increases agni, improves digestion, increases tastiness of food, calms the nerves, brings confidence and relieves spasms. Salt breaks apart kapha.

Salt in excess. Too much salt can cause us to over eat because when food is exceptionally tasty, we may be tempted keep going back for more. Salt can also create soft and flabby tissues due to water retention. Excess salt can cause problems like hypertension, ulcers, acid reflux, hair loss, gray hair, wrinkles, obstinate skin rashes, thirst and an ego-centric mind.

PUNGENT

Pungent taste is balancing for kapha and increases vata and pitta. It is the taste you might think of as "spicy" or "hot" and…pungent! It has a scraping action on the tissues which is great for kapha's thick tissues while adding heat and mobility. Pungent in small doses is OK for vatas because it promotes digestion, but too much can aggravate and break down vata's delicate tissues. Pungent should be used sparingly by pittas, since they tend to overheat. Plus, pittas don't need it — they have enough hot pungent spiciness in their nature. Think of pungent as dry heat, a kapha's dream, just like the desert.

nourish

We should never feel too heavy. Even pure vatas should feel grounded by foods, but not overly heavy.

Salt gives balancing confidence for highly anxious vatas.

High blood pressure can be a problem for all doshas. Salt is heating. Heat increases pitta in the blood. That's why cutting out salt can help high blood pressure.

HOW THE SIX TASTES
AFFECT THE DOSHAS

TASTE	ELEMENTS	vata	pitta	kapha
sweet	earth + water	↓	↓	↑
sour	earth + fire	↓	↑	↑
salty	fire + water	↓	↑	↑
pungent	fire + air	↑	↑	↓
bitter	air + ether	↑	↓	↓
astringent	air + earth	↑	↓	↓

↑ up arrow is aggravating   ↓ down arrow is balancing

HOW THE SIX TASTES
AFFECT THE MIND

TASTE	ACTION ON THE MIND	OVERINDULGENCE
sweet	compassion, satisfaction	attachment, posessiveness
sour	discrimination, stimulating	envy, jealousy, anger
salty	confidence, zest	greed, over-ambition
pungent	bold, outspoken	anger, violence, hatred
bitter	dissatisfaction, isolation	insecurity, fear
astringent	introversion	grief, sorrow

Chart content from Kerala Ayurveda, 2008.

Pungent in balance. Pungent taste is the very best for increasing our digestive fire overall and excellent for scraping and burning away ama. It reduces congestion, improves circulation, relieves muscle tension (Tiger Balm, anyone?), dries up mucus, promotes sweating and kills worms (lovely!). Examples of pungent are ginger, black pepper, chili flakes, chili peppers, horseradish and wasabi.

Pungent in excess. Pungent taste in excess will cause more heating problems like dizziness, internal burning sensation, dry mouth/palate/lips, pain in throat, heart burn, burning urination and ulcers. Pungent taste destroys strength and complexion. Think dry, red heat (like a chili powder) as being too much of the pungent taste.

ASTRINGENT

Astringent taste is balancing for pitta and kapha, while it increases vata. Think of astringent taste as cooling and drying — it sucks out water and constricts. Astringent foods are unripe bananas, pomegranates, chickpeas, turmeric, spinach, chard, kale and other leafy greens, blueberries, cranberries, aloe, fenugreek, green tea, honey.

Astringent in balance. Great for toning the tissues, removing excess water, stops bleeding and flow, heals wounds, antibacterial, dries up moisture, constricts vessels, purifies skin, constipating, good for the skin.

Astringent in excess. Can also be very drying and cooling, similar to the bitter taste will cause depletion of the tissues and constrict circulation. It also makes body parts rigid, causes farties, pain in the heart and vata disorders.

BITTER

Bitter taste is balancing for pitta and kapha, while it increases vata. Bitter taste is cold, airy and subtle, which reaches the tissues fast because of light qualities. Bitter promotes the flavor of other tastes, kind of like a palate cleanser as it wipes the other tastes away completely. Examples of bitter are coffees, black teas, green leafy vegetables, bitter chocolates and neem (a bitter Ayurvedic herb).

Bitter in balance. The bitter taste purifies the blood, detoxifies the body, reduces fever and body temperature, is a tonic for the liver and reduces cholesterol. It also reduces thirst, fainting, worms, skin diseases, over-hydration, burning sensations and vitiation of the blood.

six tastes in our food

SWEET
rice, milk, whole grains, pastas,
sweet potatoes, avocado, dates, coconut,
sweet fruits, sugars, maple syrup

SOUR
yogurt, sour cream, sour cheeses,
citrus fruits, pickles, sauerkraut, strawberries,
fermented or vinegary foods, alcohol

SALTY
sea salt, Himalayan salt, rock salt, kelp

PUNGENT
ginger, garlic, onion, hot peppers, chili flakes,
wasabi, horseradish, sriracha sauce,
black pepper, cloves

BITTER
coffee, black tea, green leafy vegetables,
dandelion, bitter chocolate, neem, aloe

ASTRINGENT
fruit peels, unripe banana, pomegranates,
chickpeas, turmeric, spinach, chard, kale and
other leafy greens, blueberries, cranberries

Dr. Vasant Lad (1998). *The Complete Book of Home Remedies* (p. 96–98). Three Rivers Press.

Bitter in excess. Bitter can be very drying so it can deplete bodily tissues including fat, muscle, bone marrow and reproductive fluids. Bitter can cause headaches, stiffness of the shoulder, exhaustion, pain, tremors, fainting, thirst, loss of strength and reproductive ability. Bitter taste is a refrigerant and can't hold any heat. It can cause emotional "coldness" or "bitterness."

BEST TASTES FOR THE DOSHAS

Don't be discouraged by what your dosha "can or cannot" eat. We ALL need ALL tastes but we need them in different amounts. Below are the best tastes for each dosha.

> **Vata: sweet, sour, salty**
> **Pitta: sweet, astringent, bitter**
> **Kapha: pungent, astringent, bitter**

Vata: sweet, sour, salty. A vata person will be balanced by sweet, salty and sour foods. These tastes provide grounding, moistness/oiliness and warming to vata's airy, dry and chilly nature. The sweet taste builds, secures and stabilizes vata both in body and mind. It also provides an oiliness that vatas need to balance their dryness. The sour taste provides heat and produces liquidity. Salty foods provide heat and water which increases digestive fire and heat overall in vata's chilly little bod and helps keep water in. Salt also stabilizes vatas anxious nature by building confidence and stability in the nervous system.

Pitta: sweet, astringent, bitter. A pitta person will be balanced by sweet, astringent and bitter foods. The sweet taste is a good builder for pitta since they have strong agni and burn through food quickly. They need a good base or they will get hungry not long after eating. They benefit from healthy carbs and proteins while astringent and bitter foods bring coolness, tone to the tissues, and prevent pitta from gaining excess weight. Pittas tend to overeat if they are stressed out, so having astringent or bitter vegetables, fruits and green teas handy will cool the "fire" in their mind so they can focus and calm down. Therefore they won't feel the need to use food (usually sweets, like chocolate, pastries, or big sandwiches) as a crutch to de-stress. If pittas have only astringent and bitter foods without the sweet they might get acid reflux and burning in the esophagus because the nurturing, stabilizing, grounding qualities of the sweet taste are missing.

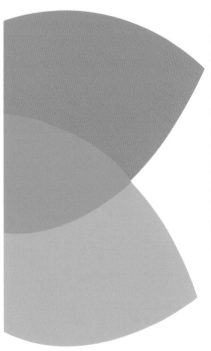

foodie

A raw diet is not recommended. Ayurveda says, give agni a boost by introducing the fire element through cooking and that way part of the job has been done already.

dosha fun

Kaphas have an affinity for taste (saliva!). They love food and take their time while savoring flavors. The key for kaphas and tastes is to reduce their quantity so they don't eat too much of the food. One large meal or two meals a day is ideal for kapha.

Kapha: pungent, astringent, bitter. A kapha person will be balanced by pungent, astringent and bitter foods. Kapha is heavy, wet, sticky and cold by nature so these tastes invoke lightness, dryness and warmth. Shed excess or low-quality tissues by lightening up, heating up and remaining fluid. Kaphas are the most mentally sound and sturdy in physical build, so they don't need a lot of stabilizing qualities in their food. If kaphas eat heavy and sticky foods like peanut butter, oatmeal, or mac 'n' cheese they will immediately feel sluggishness in their stomach. Conversely, astringent and bitter tastes will lighten and tone kapha, to keep their body and mind awake and clear.

LIFE CHECK TASTE TEST

Which tastes balance your dosha the most?

_____

_____

_____

_____

Which tastes do you currently eat the most?

_____

_____

_____

_____

Which taste is missing from your diet?

_____

_____

_____

_____

What foods can you start eating more of to get that taste in your diet?

_____

_____

_____

_____

foodie

When milk is referred to in Ayurveda, it is traditionally raw (if you have never tasted raw milk, it's so yum!). Organic non-homogenized whole milk is next best and is what I drink.

dosha fun

Kapha people are usually very sweet. They like sweet foods which can make them overly sweet — a little too sticky or clingy.

Pitta people can get a little salty. If pittas eat too many salty and spicy foods it may cause them to be ego-centric.

Vata people can be bitter. If vatas eat too many astringent and bitter foods, it leaves them cold and rigid in personality.

9
MEAL-PLAN

Mealtime

Knowledge of the six tastes and their actions on the body is essential for this next step in creating our own meals. The two biggest players in Ayurvedic cooking and meal-balancing are: doshas and the six tastes. As the chart on page 127 highlights, certain tastes benefit certain doshas. If it's clear as day, you've done a fantastic job of learning. However, at some point, you will be eating with other people. You probably don't eat solo all the time, so what happens when one meal has to feed several people? What if they are all different dosha-types and as and sitting around the same table?

This is when we put our "Ayurvedic super smarts" hat on. First of all, we don't have to make separate meals. We provide a meal with a variety of tastes and options so that each person can build their plate a little differently. Let's have some fun!

MONICA B IS THROWING AN AYURVEDIC PIZZA PARTY! LIFE HAS PIZZA PARTIES AFTER ALL, SO LET'S MAKE IT AS AYURVEDIC AS POSSIBLE.

Monica B invites three guests; vata, pitta and kapha.

On the menu is:

1) A hearty green salad with leafy kale as the base, chick peas, steamed (then chilled) broccoli, carrots and green beans.

2) As a side dish, we have a toasted loaf of crusty bread a roasted garlic bulb that has been drizzled with olive oil, for schmearing on the bread.

3) The pizza has a medium-thick crust with olive oil brushed on and topped with fresh mozzarella cheese, basil from the garden, and garden-fresh tomato slices.

4) Condiments include olive oil, chili flakes, sunflower seeds, ranch dressing and balsamic vinaigrette dressing.

HOW WILL THEY BUILD THEIR PLATES?

Kapha, knowing they need a lighter fare, would pile half their plate with salad and add some balsamic vinagrette. They will take one slice of pizza and sprinkle hot pepper flakes on it. They might also steal a garlic clove (or three) and schmear it on their pizza. They would skip the extra bread because the crust of the pizza is enough. Too much bread makes them feel heavy.

Pitta would pile 1/3 of their plate with salad and dressing. Because they have a hearty appetite, they might have two pieces of pizza, but they would skip the chili flakes. They would enjoy a piece of toasted bread with olive oil, but would bypass the garlic since it gives them heartburn.

Vata would skip the salad, or at the very least, pick out the chick peas and broccoli since it tends to make them tooty. They will go right for the bread, adding some olive oil, and might have a little garlic schmear to warm them up. They will have one slice of pizza, that they pick at, since they filled up on bread.

The result. Everyone had a great time at the pizza party. Kapha felt joyful, light, clear-headed and extra happy because of the vegetables, and not too much heaviness from cheesy pizza or bread. Pitta was content, full of humor and wit because the bitter greens helped their mind stay clear and emotions cool. They didn't get heartburn from an overly spicy pizza and avoided burping up garlic. Vata was hugging everyone and telling stories with their hands flinging in the air — for once they were not bloated! Instead, they were grounded and satisfied from a little salad, bread and pizza. Vata was able to sneak in some extra oil from the olive oil.

By knowing themselves and by adhering to right choices and right action, these three left Monica B's pizza party feeling happy and satisfied. None of them will have digestive problems tonight. They will all wake up in the morning happy with THEMSELVES for making the right choices for their bodies. Based on such a positive experience, they are likely to use their smarts to practice customizing their plates all the time.

Now, let's journey deeper into each dosha's meal plan, including the foods that balance them most, some menu ideas, and how to build their plate on a daily basis.

VATA FOODS

Oil is Vata's #1 food

"Yes" foods for vata are moist, grounding, building, nourishing, oily/fatty, easy-to-digest and warming. Think: warm, goopy, soupy, sticky, comfort foods.

Rice, grains, ghee, whole milk, cheese, citrus fruits, baked fruit, mango, coconut, cooked veggies, beets, squash, sweet potato, avocado, walnuts, almonds, cashews, dates, prunes, healthy oils (ghee, olive, coconut, flax, etc.), soups, stews, noodle dishes, rice bowls. Veggies should almost always be cooked.

"No" foods for vata are light, dry, crunchy, cold, iced, carbonated and anything gas-producing or hard to digest.

Brown rice, "extra high fiber" grains, crackers, popcorn, pretzels, raw veggies, soy products, lentils, beans, sprouts, peanuts, candy, fake sugars, bubbly water, soda, coffee, heavy meats.

Vatas favor the tastes: sweet, sour, salty

foodie

Vata does best when their food is cooked together in one pot.

Veggies should almost always be cooked for vatas.

Despite the "no" foods, vatas really love crunchy foods and must have them once in a while to satisfy the mind.

foodie

Brown rice is really no bueno for anyone, although some pittas can handle it. It is very hard to digest for vatas and kaphas and sticks in their digestive systems like glue. Best to stick with basmati rice for easier digestion. No more glue.

VATA PLATE

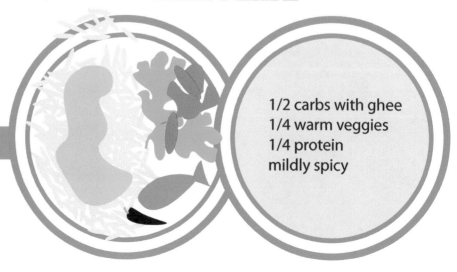

1/2 carbs with ghee
1/4 warm veggies
1/4 protein
mildly spicy

VATA MENU IDEAS

Breakfast
- Oatmeal cooked with raisins, peeled almonds,* ghee and cinnamon
- Cream of wheat, made with whole milk, add sprinkle of cardamom, cinnamon, maple syrup and dates
- Baked apples or pears, with ghee and cinnamon

Lunch/Dinner**
- Creamy asparagus soup and warm roll with butter
- Grilled cheese grilled with tomato soup
- Pasta with stir fried veggies, drizzled with olive oil and garlic sauce
- Sautéed veggies in oil or ghee, drizzled with warm pesto
- Roasted/fried vegetables such as beets, butternut squash, zucchini and sweet potatoes, roasted with olive oil and rosemary, sprinkle with salt and pepper

Snacks
- 1–2 handfuls of one thing: raisins or almonds
- Almond butter and small bread roll
- Dates rolled in shredded coconut
- Fig or date bar and glass of warm whole, organic milk
- Hummus and pita, drizzled with olive oil, add olives
- Baked apples or pears in ghee, with cinnamon

* Soak almonds in water overnight and the peels will slip off in the morning
** Cook one thing for lunch and eat the rest for dinner or vice versa

foodie

Trail mix could give vatas a tummy ache. It is best to stick with a handful of one single thing. The next day have something different to "mix" it up.

Baking fibrous fruits like apples or pears brings out their juices or waters, which is awesome for vata.

Raw foods aggravate vata causing anxiety, nervousness and dryness in the body. This makes the nutrition unavailable to our bodies even though it may be present in the food.

Leftovers and frozen foods are not recommended in Ayurveda. They lack prana and can aggravate the doshas. When possible, foods should be cooked fresh. However due to our lifestyle, that may not be possible. As a second best, cook a big dinner and have it for lunch the next day.

PITTA FOODS

Ghee is pitta's #1 food

"Yes" foods for pitta are grounding, sustaining, cooling, calming, dry. Pasta, quinoa, basmati rice, barley, wheat, ghee, whole milk, lassi, soft cheeses, all sweet fruits, dried fruits, sunflower seeds, peeled almonds,* coconut, most veggies, squashes, potatoes, sweet potatoes, peas, legumes, coconut oil, olive oil, white meats, freshwater fish.

"No" foods for pitta are salty, sour and pungent (spicy). Naturally sweet foods are good for pitta but refined sugars are not.

Sour/acidic fruits, tomatoes, eggplant, radishes, jalapeños, garlic, cayenne pepper, sour/aged cheeses, alcohol (limit it), refined white sugar, red meat, fermented and overly salty foods.

Pittas favor the tastes: sweet, astringent, bitter

* Soak almonds in water overnight and the peels will slip off in the morning

---

truth

Pittas, I know you. Just because there are "no" foods does not mean you are banned for life. Don't write me a note saying you are not giving up red meat (Ha! Yes, I've had that happen). Simply pay attention to the "no" foods and limit them. At minimum, pay attention to how they affect your body and mind if you do eat them. Most likely, you will notice that your body and emotions might not do so well and that is a sign, to omit or significantly reduce these foods. OK? Love you! *smooch*

dosha fun

Almost all my pitta friends hate tomatoes. By design maybe?

Pittas love spicy foods, so while it is not the best for them, they will have to have it sometimes or they will get mentally unstable, plus they need it to keep agni balanced.

PITTA PLATE

1/3 carbs with ghee
1/3 veggies
1/3 protein
mild or no spice

PITTA MENU IDEAS

Breakfast
- Egg white scramble sautéed with ghee, some veggies, add toast or wrap in flatbread. Sprinkle with fresh coriander (cilantro).
- Wheat/cinnamon raisin bagel or toast with almond butter and fig spread
- Oatmeal with milk, add cardamom, raisins (no sulfur) and a dab of raw organic honey on top. Optional: stir in some almond butter.

Lunch/Dinner**
- Salad with bitter greens, teriyaki salmon or chicken, lots of veggies, avocado. Add dinner roll with ghee.
- Quinoa bowl with chicken, add kale, broccoli, carrots, sprinkle with sunflower seeds
- Veggie wrap. Sauté your favorite veggies in ghee (potatoes, zucchini, broccoli, cauliflower, etc.). Add-ons: bitter greens, cottage cheese, chickpeas wrap in a flatbread or flour tortilla.
- Soft tacos with chicken or freshwater fish, black beans, corn, cilantro

Snacks
- Lassi (recipe p. 153)
- Fruit smoothie (no dairy, but add mint as a treat!)
- Dates rolled in shredded coconut
- Fig bar and a handful of almonds with a cool glass of whole, organic milk
- Seasonal fruit
- Hummus and pita or veggie sticks
- Pomegranate juice and slices of fresh coconut or mango

** Same type of foods, but dinner is a smaller portion

ayur-tip

Adding low-salt nuts or legumes to any dish will bulk it up if a pitta tends to get extra hungry and are good substitutes for meat if you are vegetarian.

Making food into a wrap goes a long way for pitta. They can load up with yummy veggies and proteins while enjoying the grounded satisfaction from the wrap.

Honey is kapha's #1 food

learn

Never heat honey. Raw cane sugar can be used in warm drinks and foods as a sweetener.

nourish

If you are not hungry in the morning, skipping breakfast is OK for all doshas. Instead, have some ginger tea or a spicy chai.

resource

For more recipes with rice noodles, go to **101cookbooks.com** and search *"rice noodles."*

"Yes" foods for kapha are light, dry, well spiced, warm, and easy to digest. Favor a vegetarian diet.

Quinoa, barley, corn, buckwheat, toasted bread, rice noodles, soba noodles, basmati rice, crackers, all legumes/lentils, all veggies, goat cheese, cranberries, raisins, apples, pears, pomegranates, berries, pumpkin seeds, sunflower seeds, popcorn, raw honey, stevia

"No" foods for kapha are salty, sour and sweet. Comfort foods will leave kapha feeling heavy and lethargic.

Citrus fruits, pineapple, banana, dates, coconut, avocado, tomatoes, dairy, white sugar, red meat, fish, overly salty foods, fried and oily foods, soda, candy, iced drinks.

Kaphas favor the tastes: pungent, astringent, bitter

KAPHA PLATE

1/2 warm,
well-spiced veggies
1/4 carbs, little ghee
1/4 light protein
spicy

KAPHA MENU IDEAS

Breakfast

- OK to skip breakfast if you are not hungry (this goes for all doshas)
- Enjoy a spicy chai (almond milk) or ginger tea use raw cane sugar as a sweetener
- Honey, cranberry jam or orange marmalade on dry and cooled toast
- Warm quinoa cereal. Once cooked, add almond milk, sprinkle cinnamon, cardamom, and a little cane sugar taste

Lunch/Dinner*

- Pesto veggies. Sauté favorite veggies with pesto (light on the oil), sprinkle with sunflower seeds
- Quinoa veggie bowl. Add steamed kale, broccoli, cauliflower, carrots, sprinkle with sunflower seeds, sprinkle the spicy mix (recipe p. 155)
- Pile veggies on quinoa and drizzle with spicy curry sauce (not too salty)
- Spicy rice noodles with bok choy, edamame, ginger-garlic sauce and chilli-pepper paste
- Soft tacos with stir fried vegetables, black beans, corn, cilantro leaves
- Barley and vegetable soup

Snacks

- Fresh veggie juices (if juice is sweet, add spice like carrot ginger or apple ginger)
- Kale chips with garlic powder
- Popcorn
- Spicy chai or ginger tea
- One type of fruit cut up in a bowl (bonus: add a squeeze of lime and cayenne pepper)
- Veggie sticks with white bean dip. (optional: add Tabasco or sriracha)
- Baked apples or pears with cinnamon, cloves, and/or anise

*Same type of foods, dinner is a smaller portion

TIP: It is best to avoid sweets. But I know you, kaphas. If you "accidentally" eat foods on the sweet or heavy side, always balance it with something spicy. For example, mango with cayenne pepper and lime; carrot apple ginger juice; or chilis in your dark chocolate. You're welcome.

---

dosha fun

Kaphas will do well with an asian-esque cuisine of light spicy sauces, veggies, and rice noodles.

Kaphas do love their sweets and it's hard for them not to have sweets. They are sooo sweeeeet. While it is not the best for them, they will have to have it sometimes or the mind will be upset.

Kaphas would benefit from "Indian Lemonade" before each meal as an appetizer.

Indian lemonade is a blend of fresh grated ginger, a squeeze of lemon and a touch of salt. Make enough to fill a small container and keep in the fridge. Eat 1/4 tsp before meals.

List what foods currently make you feel bad. Examples: indigestion, heart burn, bloating, gassiness, sits like a "rock" in your gut, moodiness, surge and crash.

_____
_____
_____
_____
_____
_____
_____
_____
_____
_____

OK. Omit these foods or only have on rare occasion. Your body is telling you these foods do not serve you.

What foods make you feel nice? Examples: Content, satisfied, well nourished, toned, easy to digest, peace of mind, light, full of energy.

_____
_____
_____
_____
_____
_____
_____
_____

Sounds like you should have more of these kinds of foods on a regular basis. Your body and mind likes them, do they balance your dosha?

_____
_____

AYURVEDIC PANTRY

In order to make super delicious Ayurvedic meals and teas, you'll need to have the right spices and ingredients in your Ayurvedic pantry. Make sure the spices are fresh and use them often, not only because you don't want to waste them but because their various tastes are super important to balance our minds and bodies.

If we have the right ingredients in our pantry, creations are endless and our mind can rest knowing we already have everything on hand. Conversely, if we have a reactive approach to eating by grabbing meals here and there, we will have to keep reinventing our endless search for food. And that stresses us out. Keep the basics in your house and you're good. Then you can make anything.

Monica B's Ayurvedic shopping list:

- ☐ BASMATI RICE
- ☐ BLACK PEPPER BALLS
- ☐ CARDAMOM: GREEN PODS AND POWDER
- ☐ CINNAMON POWDER AND STICKS
- ☐ CLOVES
- ☐ CORIANDER: SEEDS AND FRESH LEAVES
- ☐ CUMIN SEEDS
- ☐ FENNEL SEEDS
- ☐ GARLIC
- ☐ GINGER ROOT AND POWDER

- ☐ GHEE
- ☐ HING (ASAFOETIDA)
- ☐ HONEY, ORGANIC AND RAW
- ☐ LEMONS, LIMES
- ☐ MUNG DAHL (SPLIT YELLOW, NOT GREEN AND WHOLE)
- ☐ NUTMEG
- ☐ OATMEAL OR CREAM OF WHEAT
- ☐ SALT — BLACK, HIMALAYAN, SEA SALT
- ☐ TURMERIC

universal medicine

In Ayurveda, ginger is considered universal medicine because it increases agni, and almost all diseases are caused by weak agni.

Turmeric opens all seven chakras which is why it is put between the eyebrows in Indian tradition.

learn

Hing is a highly potent Indian spice used in very small doses. I will not lie — hing is very stinky to Westies' noses. Keep in a plastic bag, in Tupperware, in the garage. Just kidding. Amazing little ingredient, but it smells bad.

ayur-tip

Pods or whole spices will need to be crushed with a spoon or mortar and pestle to release their oils and get the full benefit of the whole spice.

How to use the pantry items

learn

Spices are powerful. They are added to make food taste good, but also to aid digestion and balance doshas.

Pittas be careful of too much black pepper because it is very heating.

learn

Why is it important for vata to move downwards? Because the flow of our bodies should be top to bottom. Flow starts in the mouth and goes out the rear. If the flow is wrong, we will have stagnation, clogs, and rogue flow of vata, which is imbalance.

Basmati rice

Basmati rice is traditional Indian rice and is the rice used with mung dahl in kitchari. Basmati rice is very easy to digest and tridoshic because it is grounding enough for vata and pitta and light enough, even for kapha to digest well without being too heavy or sticky. Keep it on hand for quick batches of kitchari and any other rice dish.

Black pepper balls

Decreases vata and kapha, increases pitta.

How to use: Sprinkle on foods or boil in teas for added pungent heat.

Good for: Increasing digestive fire, lightly remove/scrape toxins, helps melt chest congestion.

Cardamom pods and powder

Decreases all doshas, increases pitta in excess.

How to use: Add as an ingredient in homemade chai, sprinkle on desserts, oatmeal or rice.

Good for: Stimulates digestion, stops coughing and hiccups, prevents asthma, directs vata downward, alleviates intestinal spasms and pain.

Cinnamon powder and sticks

Decreases vata and kapha, increases pitta.

How to use: Boil sticks for teas, use powder in foods like oatmeal and sweet or savory rice dishes.

Good for: Helps increase circulation, warms the body, increases appetite, reduces gas, removes ama, reduces mucus.

Cloves powder and whole

Decreases vata, pitta and kapha.

How to use: Boil in teas, use in combination with ginger and ghee for "spicy" cookies (p. 155).

Good for: Stops hiccups and coughs, stimulates appetite, relieves bloating and gas, clove oil is a topical pain reliever for teeth and gums.

Coriander seeds and leaves (a.k.a. cilantro)

Decreases vata, kapha and especially pitta.

How to use: The leaves add a cooling effect to tacos or as a topping on kitchari. Also blend into a paste and apply topically for burning rashes or sunburn.

Good for: The seeds can be used as a digestive aid and cleanser in CCF tea (p. 152).

Cumin seeds and powder

Decreases all doshas, can aggravate pitta.

How to use: Seeds help calm and clean the digestive tract, alleviate bloating and gassiness, increase agni and digest ama. Powder can be used with lentils or beans (think, burrito) to reduce the toots and bloaties!

Good for: Keeping vata's motion downward, increasing agni, digesting toxins.

Sebastien Pole, *Ayurvedic Medicine* (Churchill Livingstone: Elsevier, 2006)

Fennel seeds

Tridoshic, benefits all doshas.

How to use: Sauté and add to tomato sauce, omelettes, and veggies. To add sweetness and digestive happiness, boil the seeds for 15 minutes and make fennel tea, eat seeds as a digestive after meals.

Good for: Digestive upsets, bloating, cramping or heart burn, helps colic in babies, relieves nervous tension.

Garlic bulb and cloves

Decreases kapha, too much will increase pitta and deplete vata.

How to use: Oh, come on, it's garlic. You've got this. Add to soups, sauces, hummus, gazpacho, and add one million other things here. If you roast it, garlic gets sweeter which is better for vatas and pittas.

Good for: Stoking digestive fire, clearing ama and heavy, sticky mucus, reduces feelings of cold, aids in fighting fevers and colds.

Note: Dried garlic powder or flakes will likely give pitta heartburn and vata the toots.

Ginger root and powder

Decreases vata and kapha, increases pitta. In Ayurveda, ginger is known as universal medicine.

How to use: Use raw ginger with garlic and sauté and add to foods. Eat a small piece (size of your pinkie fingernail) of raw ginger to stop abdominal cramping/gas instantly. Use powder in cookies, desserts or teas. Sip ginger tea to remove ama.

Good for: Melting ama and destroying toxins, clearing colds, congestion and phlegm.

Note: Fresh ginger is hot and pungent. Dry ginger is warming and sweet.

Ghee

Because it's so special, it has a special section on page 146.

Hing (asafoetida)

Decreases vata and kapha, increases pitta.

How to use: Indians use it a lot in cooking. I only use it in kitchari because I...don't know what else to do with it.

Good for: Increasing agni, melting ama, cramps, gas, stagnation in the guts.

Honey: organic, raw

Decreases vata and kapha, increases pitta.

How to use: Melt it in teas, never heat it. Drizzle on a lemon slice for a "sickness" dessert. Drizzle on fruit or toast. Never mix with ghee!

Good for: Clearing congestion, increasing agni, digesting toxins.

Note: Honey has prabhava (special quality) so although it seems wet and sweet, the effect on the body is dry, heating and scraping.

---

ayur-tip

If you have the toots, are bloated, or have tummy cramps, eat a piece of raw ginger the size of your pinky finger nail. Sprinkle with salt, chew it up. Your pains will be gone in 15 minutes or less.

---

food

Asian foods usually have a combination of garlic and ginger in their sauces which is great for all doshas and expecially for kapha.

Garlic may help reduce cholesterol and opens channels to promote proper flow.

---

learn

Prabhava means 'special quality.' Meaning, what you see is not what you get. Honey has prabhava because while it seems heavy, sticky and sweet, it actually digests dry, heating and scraping. That's probably why honey has always been used in teas as a sweetener when we have a cold.

---

oh my gheeness!
what exactly is ghee?

ghee facts!

Ghee and honey in equal portions is poison! When I asked my teacher what combo is OK, he said it's a bit complicated for the lay person, so just avoid it all together.

We crave ghee when our bodies need it. When we no longer need it, ghee loses its appeal.

Ghee has a cooling effect on us but still increases digestive fire!

Ghee has a high smoke point, so you can use it for cooking and stir-frying.

Ghee helps us reach optimal weight. If we are under weight, ghee will help us gain weight. If we need to lose weight, ghee will help us do that, too.

Ghee is a sattvic food; it promotes total harmony in the body-mind.

Ghee is the purest oil derived from buttermilk or butter. The sugar, water and salts, have been boiled off, leaving only the oil — pure fat. It looks like butter, but it's more yellow, even more buttery smelling and comes in a glass jar because it melts and solidifies depending on the temperature in the room.

Important note: People who have ama or a white tongue, should not eat ghee until their tongue is pink. **Another important note:** Too much ghee can cause ama.

Why is it good for us? Our bodies need fat — it's essential to our vitality, intelligence, digestion, happiness (fat keeps us happy), and strength. When we eat good amounts of fat, it tastes good going down and replenishes our tissues, therefore we are satisfied and truly nourished. When our taste buds are satisfied, we actually eat less! As a major bonus, ghee is an excellent aid for digestion since it is the only oil that increases agni. Yes, it's like magic! Ghee actually helps us digest and assimilate our food better.

Ghee aids the body in absorbing nutrients while "buttering" the body's insides to keep everything running smoothly. It will help us poop regularly, improves memory and lubricates the connective tissues. It's also great used on the skin as a moisturizer, or on the scalp. Ghee can be used on minor burns (non-broken skin only) to stop pain in an instant and no scarring!

Are ghee and butter the same? Nope.

- Ghee melts at room temperature and absorbs through the skin and into our tissues. Butter does not absorb and creates a film/coating.
- You can use ghee on a minor burn, but not butter
- Ghee increases digestive fire and helps us assimilate food, butter does not
- Ghee is cooling, used to cool inner and outer heat
- Ghee has a much higher smoke point than butter and does not burn easily

How to use ghee.
Spread it. Melt it. Sauté with it. Drizzle on pasta or rice. Drizzle on popcorn. Use in place of margarine in baking.

How does ghee affect the doshas?
Vata. Ghee is oleating and calming for vata and stokes digestive fire. Vatas need the oil and agni boost from ghee.

Pitta. Ghee is soothing and cooling for pitta, good for cooling a heated mind or emotions. Ghee is the food of choice for pittas.

Kapha. Ghee increases digestive fire so kaphas can use a small amount. Kaphas need just a smidge of ghee because they are already oily and cool.

Where to buy it? Good news, more and more grocery stores are carrying ghee. In 2008, I could not find a jar on a shelf at a regular grocery store and now there are a few brands to choose from. You can get it at Whole Foods, Trader Joes and **Amazon.com**. Two of my favorite brands are Pure Indian Foods and Purity Farms. You can also make it yourself (recipe p. 153). Choose the best option for the time and money you have.

The best ghee in my humble opinion is Pure Indian Foods, **pureindianfoods. com**. They even have a variety of ghee flavors like garlic or cinnamon. The owners, Sandeep (I call him "the Ghee Man") and his family, have been making organic grass-fed ghee for five generations in New Jersey. If you want the gold standard of ghee, that's the one. Other brands are good too, so don't be overly ghee-conscious. But if you wanted to know the best, that's the one. Tell them Monica B sent you!

• • • • • • • • •

more ghee facts!

Ghee has a mild laxative effect which can sometimes exit pittas back door a little quickly.

No need to refrigerate. Ghee will solidify and liquify as the temperature in the room changes and that's OK! It does get rancid over time, so don't constrain yourself, eat it up.

Keep your ghee clean. Don't go spreading ghee on your toast and then dip the crumby knife back in the ghee. Spoon out a separate amount and use. No double dipping, no crumbs in the ghee!

• • • • • • • • •

Mung dahl

You'll need these little yellow split guys for kitchari or anytime you are feeling mentally or physically "off." Mung dahl is a sattvic, complete protein and very easy to digest. It is the accompanying ingredient in kitchari along with basmati rice. Together, the two make a filling, satisfying, comforting, yet tri-doshic and easy to digest meal for the whole family (I tried to make that sound like a commercial).

Nutmeg powder

Decreases vata and kapha, increases pitta.

How to use: In desserts, in spinach dishes, teas, and sprinkle in warm milk with cardamom for as a sleep aid.

Good for: Increasing appetite, insomnia or interrupted sleep, calms intestinal pain, spasms and bloating.

Salt, Himalayan

Decreases vata, increases kapha and pitta.

How to use: To make foods tasty, dissolve in warm water and gargle, dissolve completely and use with neti pot.

Good for: Stimulating appetite to prime us for digestion, clears obstructed channels, increases kapha and mucus, moves vata downwards.

Turmeric powder

Decreases kapha, increases pitta and vata in excess. Turmeric stains everything yellow.

How to use: Make a paste with milk and put on zits! Add to rice, veggie, and curry dishes. Add to dips. Put it on minor cuts, cover with a Band-Aid.

Good for: Purifying the blood and liver, antibacterial, stops bleeding, helps skin problems.

DIGESTIVES

All of the pantry spices affect digestion, whether to kindle agni, relieve bloating and cramping and/or digest ama. In Ayurveda, the most common root cause of disease is a result of mal-digestion and almost all of these spices help that in some way. So, how many of these spices do YOU use daily? No judging, just awareness. Let's work to get some of these spices in your diet. Another thing to notice is that most of these spices balance/decrease vata and kapha because those two doshas have low agni. If pitta went crazy with the spices, they would get imbalanced.

Sebastien Pole, *Ayurvedic Medicine* (Churchill Livingstone: Elsevier, 2006)

AYURVEDIC EATING IS NOT GENERALIZED IT IS PERSONALIZED

What about coffee?!

Did you really think I would forget about Westies and their coffee? Authentic Ayurveda says that we should not have coffee because of the caffeine. Caffeine is an addictive drug (sorry!), it constricts flow, makes you pee which causes dehydration, can cause headaches and make us manic/anxious. Yes, we all know that. And, there's a coffee shop on every corner! I know you…you're going to have your coffee regardless of what I or Ayurveda say. So I'll work with you a little bit and give you the best coffee-making combinations for each dosha.

AYURVEDIC QUALITIES

Coffee has a bitter (cold, dry and light) taste, which is imbalancing for vata, but balancing for pitta and kapha. The bitter taste is a blood purifier, detoxifies the body, liver tonic and depletes tissues, especially reproductive tissues. Coffee could be a vata's worst enemy because it has the exact same qualities as vata. On the flip side, coffee will cool pitta, while it dries and uplifts kapha.

CUSTOMIZE YOUR CUP O' JOE!

Vata coffee. Vatas need lots of warm milk in their coffee for balance. Start with 1/2 mug of warm milk and add brown or turbinado sugar, stir, then add 1/2 mug of coffee. If the coffee is strong, add warm water to your milk and then a splash of coffee. This way you get a taste of the coffee, but overall this is a nourishing, calming drink for vata without sending anxieties through the roof. As a MEGA-BONUS, vatas can add ghee to their coffee! Vata coffee should always be warm. This is how I make my coffee.

Pitta coffee. Pittas will also be balanced by vata coffee as they benefit from the sweet taste in milk and sugar. Pittas can handle a slightly darker coffee with a little less milk. They won't get as anxious as vata with stronger coffee because pittas are more sturdy. The people who are angry or crabby before their morning coffee are likely pitta people, because they need the bitter taste in coffee to "cool" them down. Pittas can also have an iced coffee during summer. Also, as a MEGA-BONUS, pittas can add ghee to their coffee, too!

Kapha coffee (how fun is that to say). Kaphas will feel uplifted from coffee, rather than manic like vata. Kaphas need a little kick in the pants because they don't like to move. They can enjoy a stronger coffee, but it should have less milk. Milk and sugar are not friends for kapha. The heaviness and sweet taste will have them craving sweets all day long. If kaphas need a sweetener, they can use honey. Mind you, kaphas would love to tip the sugar shaker and hold for 1, 2, 3, 4, 5+ seconds until their drink tastes like candy. But, if kaphas use the bitter taste in coffee to their advantage, they can get the energy they need without the sugar spike and crash. Kaphas will gag at the thought of putting ghee in their coffee.

COFFEE SPICE COUNTER
Cardamom. Reduces the effects of caffeine, warming, digestive.
Cinnamon. Tri-doshic. Not for pitta in summer.
Brown sugar. Sweet. Good for vata and pitta.
Honey. Qualities are drying, heating and scraping. Good for kapha.
Nutmeg. Aphrodisiac, heating. Good for vata and kapha.

YUMMY COFFEE SUBSTITUTES
Rajas, from Maharishi. This is a nice cup of fake joe. You have to boil it for 5 minutes for full potency — you cannot steep it like tea.
Ayurvedic Coffee Roast. Another great cup of fake joe that has a couple Ayurvedic herbs in it (ashwaghanda and shatavari), which help ground and stabilize. Order on **Amazon.com**.
Chai. Make it at home (recipe p. 153)!

RECIPE: GHEE COFFEE
Good for vatas and pittas
- Warm whole milk or coconut milk on the stove.
- Add a teaspoon of ghee
- Whisk together while you sing something fun for 1 minute
- It will be foamy
- Add 4–6 ounces coffee to the happy foamy goodness

Monica B's recipes

Now that you're pantry is stocked up, here are some Ayurvedic recipes I use all the time. Since food is our medicine, you can incorporate them into your regular diet and some are even helpful when you are feeling sick.

DRINK RECIPES

tips

Don't worry about making home made tea too strong because you can always dilute it with water.

Cough tea will taste like chai. Mmm. In fact, add some cardamom and you almost have chai. Tastes so good you will not even miss the black tea bag!

CCF tea

Helps calm the guts, great for sluggish digestion, clearing ama, bloating, cramps and constipation. Best when sipped on its own and not with a lot of food.

> 1 tsp. each of cumin seeds, fennel seeds and coriander seeds

Fill teapot or saucepan with water. Boil for 10–15 minutes, let steep for stronger tea (hint: you can always dilute). Vatas and kaphas can sip while it's warm. Pittas can have room temperature or cool.

Cough tea

This spicy tea is beneficial if you have a cough (dry or wet) as well as extra mucus in your chest or throat. Also keeps ama at bay so you could sip regularly as a preventative medicine. Psst…it's really similar to chai!

> 1 tsp. crushed black pepper
> 1 tsp. crushed cloves
> 2 cinnamon sticks

Fill teapot or saucepan with water. Boil 10–15 minutes, let steep for stronger tea. Sip warm with honey (honey should not be added to super hot water).

Congestion tea

This bright, pungent tea may help liquefy mucus to relieve congestion in your chest and sinuses.

> 1/4 tsp. fresh grated ginger (1/8 for pittas)
> 1/4 tsp. turmeric
> Juice of 1/2 lime
> Honey to taste
> 1 mug of warm water

Mix the ingredients together and voila!

Monica B's chai

I concocted this recipe on my own because I was saddened by the powdery stuff at coffee shops called "chai." I swear I make the best chai. I believe the secret ingredient is black pepper which gives it a rich zing.

- 12 cardamom pods
- 8 cloves
- 8 black pepper balls
- 2 cinnamon sticks
- 1/4 tsp. of ginger
- 3 black tea bags

Crush the cardamom, cloves and pepper. Fill a pot with 3 1/2 cups water, 2 cups organic whole or coconut milk. Dump all spices in the pot. Turn on medium heat (it overflows quickly!) and bring just to a boil then remove from heat. Add 3 tea bags and let steep for 10 minutes. Strain into a mug, add brown sugar, if desired. It will be rich and milky.

Dr. Lad's lassi

Lassi's open all channels and is a digestive aid. Sip lassi during or after a meal or have as a snack!

- 2 cups water
- 1/2 part plain, full fat yogurt (1/3 cup is good to start)
- 1/4 tsp. dry ginger powder
- 1/2 tsp. cardamom
- Sugar to taste

With a whisk or hand blender, churn all ingredients for 2 minutes. It will get liquidy and frothy. Pour into a cup. Optional to sprinkle extra cardamom on the top.

FOOD RECIPES

Ghee

(Finally)! Here's that recipe we keep talking about.

Melt 1 lb. organic unsalted butter in small sauce pan on medium heat. Once the butter is melted, the butter will boil and sputter. Turn the heat down to very low. The ghee will start to bubble and crackle, making a foam — do not stir. Little bits will fall to the bottom and other crunchy bits will float to the top, forming a crust. You want the golden goodness in the middle. It should take about 15 minutes to cook.

Keep an eye on ghee, it can burn. If it smells like buttery popcorn, you're doing great. If it smells like toasted nuts and turns a little brown, you've burnt it.

Once the ghee has stopped making a popping noise and you can see clear all the way to the bottom of the pan (swipe away the foam with a spoon to look), set aside until it is just warm. Spoon off the top (toss it) and then spoon out the clear/yellow oil in the middle into a glass jar. Discard the crust on the bottom.

or, make lazy chai

Take your chai spices (doesn't matter how many of each, to keep it interesting) and crush them. Throw them in a pot of water and boil for 10 minutes. Strain into a mug with warm milk. Black tea bag is optional.

dosha fun

A hack recipe, like the one above, will drive a pitta crazy.

cook with love

Does your grandma's cooking always taste extra good, almost like she's putting magic in it? It's because she's putting love in it. She's not racing around like mom doing a million things at once and trying to toss food on the table.

Putting love in your food matters. If you cook with love, others can taste it. The energy is there and our entire being thrives from it.

personal tip

Sometimes I like to put my kitchari in a tortilla and wrap it up like an Indian burrito. Then I add some fennel bulb shavings and some sriracha sauce for a kick. Note: This would not be appropriate for the kitchari cleanse.

learn

Use organic raisins with no sulfur. Soaking raisins in water adds moisture which eases digestion and eliminates raisin gassies. Almond peels are hard to digest so soaking and removing the peels is like giving our digestion a head start.

Kitchari

Disclaimer about my recipe: Traditional Indian kitchari is better than mine. Like, Indians just smile at their kitchari and it turns out better. However! I experimented for a long time to come up with a recipe that tastes close. Don't forget the hing! I was shy about it because it's super stinky, but it makes all the difference in the dish.

1/2 cup mung dahl, split yellow lentils (not the whole green ones)
1 cup basmati rice
3 cups water (for moist/soupy, use 4 cups water)
3 tbsp. of ghee
1 inch piece of fresh ginger (root), peeled, chopped up well
1 tsp. ajwain seeds
1 tsp. fennel seeds
1 tsp. cumin seeds
3 cinnamon sticks
1/2 tsp. turmeric
1/4 tsp. hing (asafoetida)
Optional: pick two veggies. 1 cup chopped fresh carrots, cauliflower, kale, etc.

Wash mung dahl and rice until water runs clear. Heat and boil the water. Throw in the mung dal and rice. Cover. Turn heat down to low.

Crush the ajwan, fennel and cumin seeds. In another pan, heat ghee on medium and add the crushed seeds, ginger, turmeric, hing and cinnamon sticks. It should smell really good! If adding veggies, toss those in with the roasted spices.

When the water is no longer covering the mung dal & rice but there is about 1/2 water in the pot, add the spices and veggies and give a quick stir. Cover and continue to cook until all water is absorbed.

Tadaaaa! Serve with ghee and you can add a little Himalayan or black salt. Kitchari has many variations and can be adjusted with spices to be more suitable for your dosha.

World's best oatmeal

This oatmeal is a grounding breakfast for vatas and hearty for pittas. It will probably be too heavy for kaphas. It is a lovely balance of carbohydrates, protein, and fats. I ate this a lot when I was pregnant (even for dinner sometimes) because Ayurvedically speaking, this recipe will nourish all our tissues.

Slow cook oatmeal or 1 packet of instant oatmeal
7 almonds, soaked in water overnight
10–15 organic, no-sulfur, raisins, soaked overnight in water
Brown sugar
Ghee or honey

Peel the almonds. Use the raisin water to make your morning oatmeal (genius!). Add the raisins and naked almonds. Stir in a little brown sugar and ghee. Kaphas can omit the brown sugar and use honey instead of ghee (remember, never eat honey and ghee together). Also, add 1/2 banana, a handful of blueberries, 2 dates, or any combo of those. It's like an oatmeal salad!

Happy ginger spicy cookies

This recipe is a modification of Laura's Ginger Snaps. Laura was my manager in 1999 and I would beg her to make these rockin' cookies. I altered her recipe to include ghee and went heavier on the spices to give a digestive boost!

- 6 tbsp. room temperature butter
- 6 tbsp. ghee
- 1 cup brown sugar
- 1/4 cup molasses
- 1 egg
- 2 cups flour
- 1/2 tsp. salt
- 2 tsp. baking soda
- 1 tsp. cinnamon
- 1 1/2 tsp. powdered cloves
- 2 tsp. powdered ginger
- Optional: Candied ginger for the tops

Preheat oven to 350 degrees. In a mixing bowl, cream the butter, sugar, and molasses. Add egg and mix. Stir together flour, salt, baking soda, cinnamon, cloves, and ginger in separate bowl. Add flour combo to the mixing bowl and mix well. Spoon blobs onto cookie sheet and bake for 8–12 minutes (8 minutes is soft in my oven). Immediately after pulling out of the oven, place some ginger candies on the top.

Spicy oil

This recipe is from my first Ayurvedic teacher, Dr. Apte. Balances kapha and vata by adding a drizzle of heat to meals. Kaphas could drizzle on popcorn.

- 1 cup cooking oil
- 1 tbsp. brown or black mustard seeds
- 1 1/2 tbsp. cumin seeds
- 1 tsp. hing (asafoetida)
- 1 1/2 tbsp. turmeric

Heat the oil in a small pot. Add 2–3 mustard seeds and then they pop, the oil is hot. Remove the pot from the heat and add the rest of the mustard seeds. Cover while they pop. Then add cumin seeds, hing and turmeric. Allow oil to cool for 5 minutes. Pour in a glass jar and store at room temperature. Drizzle on steamed veggies, rice or pasta dishes, use as spread or condiment.

food

If a recipe calls for Crisco® or margarine, use ghee as a substitute. You'll turn it from craptastic to fantastic!

tip

You can alter the spices in any recipe to be more friendly for your dosha(s).

Adding ghee causes some cookies to turn to mush or crumbles. You might have to experiment a little and when you perfect it, write it down, then send to me and I'll post for all of us to use!

Incompatible foods

In Ayurveda, there are certain food combinations that should be avoided. Remember one of the causes of imbalance is mistaken intellect? This is a great example of how we might not know what's best for us (mistaken intellect). Let's talk about these food combinations that just don't mesh well.

Dairy and fruit. Fruit sours and curdles the milk in our stomachs.

Dairy and fish. No cheese on that Filet-O-Fish (*wink* I know you're not eatin' Filet-O-Fishes)! Salmon with lemon, salt and pepper is a good choice.

Dairy and meat. Too heavy, murky and way hard on digestion! Have meat with veggies.

Eggs and milk. If you have an omelet, omit the milk in your morning tea or coffee.

Fruit and fruit juice should be consumed by itself. Again, think of it as a snack.

No yogurt. Unless you turn it into lassi, yogurt clogs channels. Mango lassi is popular in Indian culture, but is not Ayurvedic.

As a general rule, milk and fruit don't really dance well with other foods. They are loners and should be consumed themselves. You can have milk with non-yeasty grains, like cereal, but no banana or strawberries on the cereal. This is especially important for kids. Try avoiding the incompatible foods on your kiddos and I bet they will get sick much less often.

The list is not all that complicated and it's pretty intuitive. Drinking milk with fish might turn our stomachs just thinking about it. Guzzling milk with pineapple seems a little strange too, right? For us Westies, the biggest challenge will be not to combine fruit and diary because that combo is everywhere. If you remain mindful remembering that fruits are eaten alone, it's easy to stick to.

PERSONALIZED EATING

Food and eating is a pretty big topic in Ayurveda so try not to get lost in too many details. If you eat at the right time and according to your dosha by choosing foods from nature that make you feel good, that is a fantastic start. Your meals will become unique as you are so plan ahead for what you need as you start to incorporate these wonderful ingredients into your meals.

why are yogurt and fruit so bad together?

Yogurt and fruit is considered a bad food combination. Fruit curdles the yogurt which turns digestion sour and rancid. The result could bring heartburn, an acidic taste in the mouth or bloating. The combo is also a channel clogger and potential ama creator. If you have digestive problems and are currently eating fruit and yogurt, omit the combo (omit yogurt all together) and see if you feel better.

more on yogurt

Yogurt clogs channels, but the properties change when unsweetened yogurt is churned with at least an equal quantity or more of water. It turns into a buttermilk or lassi which conversely opens channels, promoting proper flow. Great for all doshas to aid digestion especially when digestive spices are added.

10
MOVE-MEANT

Break a sweat!

not too much cardio, vata

Anything too cardio intensive will increase the already swift motion in vatas mind-body, which will create more movement and craving for movement and then vata will fly away like a kite with no string.

Many vatas love to run, and understandably because it's so natural for them. They can stride effortlessly like gazelles (gazelles are vata!), but it's not the best exercise for them. If you now have a pout face cause I told you not to run, hear me out. It's all about balance, right? If you are a vata and running makes you feel amazing, please make sure to:

a) limit the distance or you could tax your delicate joints

b) balance running with a good amount of stretching and add yoga a couple times a week

c) get new shoes every 6–9 months to keep it cushy on the joints

d) do abhyanga regularly

If you notice any vata-type symptoms from running like anxiety, emotional roller coaster, bloating, gas, scattered mind, sore joints, you might want to reconsider running as your primary exercise.

EXERCISE IN AYURVEDA

Would you be surprised if I told you that a good exercise session is 30 minutes long and considered complete so long as you broke a sweat in your pits and on your brow? This is how Ayurveda views exercise as beneficial. It's not about how tight you can make your booty or how ripply your arms look. Instead, Ayurveda says exercise should be used to increase agni, improve circulation, remove toxins through sweat and keep our tissues toned. Exercise can also be calming for the mind especially if we exercise outdoors as much as possible. Our bodies love nature. Because we *are* nature, right?! Whenever we can and as much as we can (daily and you get a gold star), take it outside and move your body to break a light sweat every day for at least 30 minutes.

Exercises for vata. There is no other dosha that likes to move as much as a vata so you would think exercise would be easy, quite natural for them. And, yes, that's true. Ironically vatas need to consciously slow their normally speedy pace when exercising. Like increases like and vata energy is movement, therefore too much movement will create too much vata. They are naturally jumpy, wiggly, constantly running their mind, and inconsistent. An exercise routine that brings more motion will create that kinetic energy in them *all* the time. What they really need is strength, flexibility and stillness. Vatas benefit most from exercise that is scheduled, steady, grounded and moving from intention.

Anything that promotes keeping both feet on the ground is a pretty good exercise for vata. Grounded, people! Vatas need a nice balance of strength and flexibility because they have less muscle mass and their dry nature has a tendency to make the body stiff or brittle. Moderate strength training will build their muscles and provide stamina (vatas also tend to be klutzy. They are the most graceful ballet dancers, but will trip over their own feet when walking). Using their own weight to train as in yoga, pilates, ballet-inspired and barre classes are perfect. This makes the workout challenging enough without exhausting vata, gives their muscle shape and tone, increases circulation, and also provides well-needed flexibility.

Exercises for pitta. They really like the physicality of exercise, so a pitta doesn't need a whole lot of motivating or coaxing to get moving. They actually seek out physical activity and competition. Pittas need to avoid exercise that is too competitive or too hot.

Pittas will do best with a combo of cardio that combines a cooling element, like cycling or swimming. Cool air and cool water will make pitta feel like they've had an awesome workout but will not overheat them. A consistent yoga practice is also very helpful to destress our pitta friends. They love to sweat and sweat quite easily. If they don't sweat in a workout they will feel it was not worthwhile. It also explains why pittas guzzle water like crazy — not only do they need to cool their heat with water, but they are constantly losing water through sweat.

Pittas can do some strength training, although they can end up feeling "heavy" as their muscles are easily sculpted. For some, they really do love the challenge of seeing how muscley they can be (AH-nold Schwarzenegger is a pitta).

Exercises for kapha. It's highly important that kaphas vigorously move and sweat. Kaphas are the hardest dosha to get into a consistent exercise regime because they lack the "mobile" quality. They have a tendency to stay steady and slow. However, just because it's not in their nature to move and wiggle, once they find an exercise routine they love, they will feel SO light, alive and energized!

You've probably guessed, but cardio is best for kapha to balance their heavy, static qualities. Cardio can range from run-walking, power walking, elliptical trainer or anything aerobic. The key for kaphas is to have a buddy! Remember, kaphas are all about love and companionship. A kapha will even feed off the energy of a lively vata or sharp pitta, which keeps them going.

Kaphas need workouts to be invigorating, enjoyable, and fun so they have something to look forward to next time. Kaphas are the pleasure seekers and pleasure exuders. If it's not fun or too physically difficult, they won't do it. Nor will they stick to a regimen if it makes them too sore/uncomfortable.

Did I mention kaphas are stubborn? Yes, hard to move and stubborn. They just need positive reinforcement from buddies around them and an activity that is fun. Daily exercise is important to keep digestive fire strong, and to induce a sweat which helps release toxins and excess water and breaks up stagnation. Kaphas, even if you do 20 minutes a day of power walking in your neighborhood, that is awesome! Just do that. Buy a pretty new pair of squishy sneakers and move your body. You will feel fantastic in no time!

not too hot, pitta

Pittas should not exercise in the sun or do hot yoga — it's just too darn hot! This could cause irritability, over-active agni, a super-charged competitive streak, or an inability to find stillness and peace in their mind. Working out under an early morning or cloudy sky with a little wind, near water, is a pitta's dream. Pittas, you can also enjoy a brisk evening walk when the sun is setting.

not too heavy, kapha

One thing that kaphas should not do is lift heavy weights. They are already quite strong and don't need to make their muscle tissue more dense. They need to lengthen and lighten their body. Kaphas are also not great runners because they are not light on their feet. So, kaphas, if you don't want to run, that's OK, just find an activity you really enjoy, like going for a hike (while wearing a heavy backpack), to reach a beautiful field of flowers.

tri-doshic exercises

Hikes
Leisurely bike ride
Brisk walk
Yoga
Pilates

EATING AND EXERCISING

Exercise after eating is one of the worst things we can do for our digestion because the food gets pushed deeper into the tissues instead of moving through the digestive tract. No bueno because that creates ama and the food is no longer used as fuel. The food has been filed away because it didn't get enough attention.

YOGA

There are many books on yoga, so this could be a whole book by itself, but in general yoga is tri-doshic but there are certain yoga practices that benefit certain doshas more than others. *Ashtanga* (power) yoga is great for kaphas because it will get their heart beating and bring on the sweaties while utilizing their natural strength. Restorative yoga is nourishing for constantly on-the-go vatas who need a coveted time and space to nourish themselves. *Hatha* or yin yoga is really good for precision pittas who like to make sure their moves are in right alignment and a workout that is challenging and sweaty. Please note, kaphas will be drawn to restorative yoga and pittas will be drawn to ashtanga yoga, however like increases like so those are not the best choices.

OVER-EXERCISING

Us Westies can have extreme views on exercise. If we are not busting our tush 3+ times a week for at least 45 minutes, we figure we may not as well bother. Am I wrong? One extreme or the other. For many of us, a daily brisk walk for 20 minutes doesn't seem like "enough" to make a physical change, right? Believe it or not, it could be just right. Remember, appropriate exercise in Ayurveda is daily and lasts for 20–30 minutes at an intensity that breaks a sweat. If you don't sweat at all, it's not enough. If you are dripping from head to toe, it's too much. A little sweat is just right.

Over-exercising may lead to increased hunger, injury, fatigue, a breakdown of tissues, and overall stress on the body. It can be just too much! Consistent exercise we can do 5–7 times a week for is best for our bodies and agni. Our body will rely on the schedule which will give our tissues daily use. As health maintenance, regular exercise will also clear our mind and help prevent stress build up.

> **Consistent exercise you can do 5–7 times a week for 20–30 minutes to break a sweat is best for our bodies and agni.**

AGNI AND EXERCISING

Exercise is one of the best ways to increase agni because it creates heat from within. However, we have to be mindful not to send agni into overdrive because it will make us super hungry and cause us to overeat. Some of you may have experienced this if you have run marathon or triathlon. You see, when we exercise with high intensity like bootcamp, cross-training, or extreme sports, our bodies will call for more fuel to maintain the hard work. If we are a professional athlete or if being physically fit is part of our day job, we truly do expend more energy and will need more food. However, most of us might workout at a very high intensity for only 2–3 days a week, which is not enough to burn off all the food agni is calling for.

Overall, keep agni strong through exercise but don't overdo it. If you find yourself constantly hungry, check your workout routine and see if you need to bring down the intensity. With practice, you'll find your perfect spot where agni, exercise, and nutrition all work together for you.

LIFE CHECK EXERCISE

What types of exercises are best for your dosha?

_____

_____

_____

What types of exercises are you currently doing?

_____

_____

_____

What exercises can you incorporate that are better for your dosha?

_____

_____

_____

Do you move your body for 30+ minutes every day?

_____

_____

If not, what is one simple thing you can do to start?

_____

_____

well-rounded exercise blends

running + yoga
strength training + swimming
barre + yoga
strength training + barre
running + barre
cross training + yoga

Monica B's favorite exercise resources

BOOKS:

Yoga as Medicine,
by *Yoga Journal* and
Timothy McCall

Beth Shaw's YogaFit,
by Beth Shaw

DVDS:

Pure Barre*

YogaFit

Pop Physique

Shiva Rae's Fluid Power
Vinyasa Flow

Beryl Bender Birch's
Power Yoga: The Practice

*if you go to one of the
Pure Barre studios in Los Angeles,
say "hi" to Marni!

ONLINE:
Yogaglow.com

Is your current exercise session too long or too intense?

_____

_____

perspective

Does the word "discipline" sound like punishment to you? I would encourage you to think about it differently. Think of discipline as adherence. Adhering to a passion. Adhering to a practice. Adhering to a habit you know will enhance your life.

you matter

Toss out the scale. Your physical body, your emotions and the way your clothes fit will be a better gauge to determine if you are at a healthy weight for YOU.

Are there any exercise blends that combine what you love *and* what is good for your dosha?

_____

_____

_____

_____

What does your NEW exercise regime look like now that you have it closer to an Ayurvedic schedule and favorable for your dosha?

Type of exercise: _____

_____

_____

_____

How many times per week and at what time? _____

_____

_____

_____

Duration: _____

_____

_____

Results: _____

_____

_____

Pranayama: breath of life

WHAT IS PRANAYAMA?

Pranayama is essentially life breath. It is the practice of extended breathing in order to supply our body with prana, which is life energy or life source. Breath is the most life-giving thing we do. When we are born we take a BIG inhale. And as we die, we take a long, slow, deep exhale.

Exercise and pranayama prep the body and mind for stillness and awakening before meditation.

Breath is the reason we are alive. But how often do we really think about it? Some yoga and meditation students are already aces, but even then, I'm sure there are stressful times when we forget to use our breath as a tool. For the non-yoga and meditation students, our breath might be completely forgotten about or taken for granted. Our bodies function on automatic in so many ways, we might just assume our breath will keep us going, with or without our mindfulness. And I suppose that's true, right? Our heart will keep going, our lungs, and the breath keep doing their thing while we keep doing our thing. Thank you heart and lungs for all you do!

Remember, the nose is the fastest passage way to the mind so as we regulate our breath, we regulate our mind, which regulates our body. Over time if we breathe fast and shallow like anxious little bunnies, our body will think we are in a constant state of panic or stress. However if we take time each day to breathe slow and deep, our mind can tell the body that all is well, no need for alarm, we are doing just fine. That's how powerful breath can be used as a therapy — and we all have the ability to do it!

WHY IS PRANAYAMA GOOD?

In using our breath as a powerful tool, we can control our bodies and minds to help reduce stress, calm the nervous system, bring clarity and peace to the mind, and weight loss to name a few reasons. Other benefits include: an energy boost, a sense of calm, builds concentration, focuses intention, and massages our internal organs while it breeds discipline and confidence.

Raise your hands if you have a regular pranayama practice. Only three of you. Well, then, this is a great time to start. Even 5–10 minutes out of your day for daily pranayama practice and you will notice a calm, more open, mind.

learn: belly breathing

On the inhale our lower bellies balloon out, and on the exhale our belly buttons go in toward the spine.

Breathing from the chest creates stress. Breathing from the belly tells the body/mind that it can relax.

did you know?

The slower you breathe, the longer you will live. Breathing slowly from the belly calms the mind and heart, reducing stress levels instilling calm and peace in the body. It will also lower blood pressure and reduce the risk of heart attack.

Pranayama literally translates to "lengthening prana."

Monica B's favorite pranayama

learn

If anyone says "sit with your chakras aligned," it means sit straight! Pretend there is an invisible string going from your butt, up your spine, and through the top of your head.

Chakras are the seven energy centers starting from the base of our spine and going up up to hover just above our head.

benefits of so hum

- Stress reduction

- Promotes relaxation and peace in the mind

- Improves mental focus and concentration

- Helps you wake up easier because it brings in prana

- Calms the nerves

- Brings total presence (so we don't worry about the future or lament the past)

- Helps relieve constipation

SO HUM

So hum is a mantra and meditation which connects our higher self or, spirit to our physical body. Practicing so hum connects the breath to the body, mind, and spirit, reminding us that all we need is ourselves because everything we really need is on the inside. When we are anxious, depressed, lonely, or stressed, it can consume us, making it a challenge to see the positive. Once we realize we have everything we could possibly need within, the mind releases.

So means, "I am." Hum means "that" or "the divine." I am that. I am the Divine.

Gosh, this always springs tears to my eyes because how often do we actually honor and love ourselves enough to say these words?

How to do so hum:

1) Sit in a comfy position, spine straight, chakras aligned. Sit either cross-legged on the floor or in a chair, back straight, chest open, both feet on the ground. If you are laying down, lay on your right side.

2) Breathe through the nose, mouth closed.

3) As you inhale slowly and deeply, think to yourself "soooooo." As you exhale, think "huuummmm." On the inhale, our lower bellies balloon out, and on the exhale, our belly buttons go in toward the spine.

Practice so hum for at least 10 minutes and go as long as you want. Set a timer so you can fully release yourself.

While practicing so hum, simply do the mantra and the breath. You may also want to visualize that you are inhaling the light of life and it is filling up your body. On the exhale, visualize all the junk (old feelings, worries, stress) flowing out. This way, we can make room for new energy, fresh and clean.

NADI SHODHANAM

Nadi shodhanam (NAH-dee-SHOW-da-num) or alternate nostril breathing is what I like to call "instant calm." There are two channels that go through our nose. One is female, and it's cooling. The other is male, and it's heating. By practicing the pranayama of nadi shodhanam, we are balancing male and female, warm and cool energies, to bring the body back to center. If we're stressed, nervous, or need some clarity of mind, nadi shodhanam will bring us back to center and calm the entire nervous system.

How to do nadi shodhanam:

Sit in a chair or on the floor, chest open, shoulders down, chakras aligned.

1) Take your right hand and cover right nostril with right thumb.

2) Exhale air all the way out, concave the belly.

3) Inhale, puff out the belly.

4) Switch and put ring finger over left nostril.

5) Exhale.

6) Switch before on the exhale.

7) Repeat 10x on each side.

Nadi shodhanam is excellent to practice before anything that might make us nervous, like a presentation at work or playing violin in front of strangers. It resets the entire system to flow along a peaceful river of neutral calm. When we can control our breath, we can control our mind and emotions. Use it as-needed for stress emergencies and/or practice daily as whole body-mind nourishment.

KAPALABHATI

Kapalabhati (Kah-PAHL-bah-tee) translates to "glowing" or "shining" skull. It purifies the mind by forcefully ridding toxins and it's a little cardio work out, too! This pranayama is awesome for infusing energy, heat, and cleaning out the cobwebs in our body-mind. It is said that the benefits of 10 minutes of kapalabhati is equivalent to a 1 hour cardio workout! This is especially excellent for people who are restricted from normal exercise.

The breathing is a series of forceful exhalations one after the other. It might feel like we are running out of breath, but don't worry, the body will automatically inhale for us. We have all heard of laughter being the best medicine. Kapalabhati works the same way. Think about laughing, "ha-ha-ha." Or, exhale-exhale-exhale. During laughter and kapalabhati we get to a deep level of exhalation, forcing toxins out, while bringing in fresh oxygen/prana.

benefits of nadi shodhanam

- Dissolves stress anxiety, tension, anger and fear
- Clearing of channels to enhance energy flow
- Releasing toxins
- Calming a busy mind
- Clarity of mind and mental grounding
- Benefits all doshas with a special affinity for vata and pitta

THE JOURNEY OF A THOUSAND MILES BEGINS WITH ONE STEP.

How to do kapalabhati:

Practice daily in the morning before breakfast and prepare to do three rounds. Start with a count of 20–30 exhales, then rest and see how you feel. If you can do more, go to 50 and build from there. Work up to 2–5 minutes.

1) Sit with legs crossed in a lotus-like position or if in a chair, both feet on the ground.

2) Spine straight, chest open, like a string is going from your butt up through the top of your head and holding you straight.

3) Using the diaphragm, inhale while ballooning the belly.

4) Start! Quick and short forceful exhales, using the diaphragm, counting, 1-2-3-4-5 (you will automatically inhale)

5) Take a rest when you are tired and repeat 3x. Work up to 2–5 minutes a day, and you will notice the benefits.

After kapalabhati you will feel energized, awake, clear. You might feel a tingly sensation in your fingers or arms as the energy moves through.

Note: The folks that do 10 minutes of kapalabhati are conditioned to do so. Feel free to work up to that, but if you feel lightheaded or dizzy, stop and rest.

benefits of kapalabhati

- Purifies the channels

- Can help weight loss

- Strengthens the respiratory system: strengthening lungs, lung capacity, purifies nasal passage and removes blockages in the chest

- Strengthens and stimulates the digestive system

- Stimulates the circulatory system. Gets the blood to all parts of the body by opening channels and promoting circulation

- Purges us of all negativity in mind, body, spirit

- Helps to overcome stress, depression and negative emotions

- Gives mental clarity

ayur-tip

If you can't do kapalabhati in the morning, make sure to do it on an empty stomach at least three hours after a meal. Otherwise, you will get a cramp and you'll go pushing food around where it doesn't belong, away from the digestive tract.

In Your Elements

11

SENSE-ATIONAL

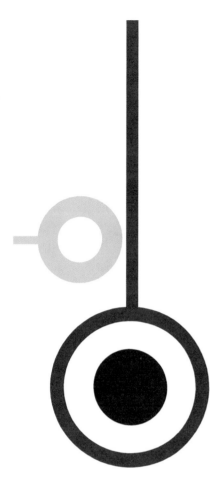

We hear. We see. We touch. We smell. We taste.

And that's it, my friends. These five miraculous senses deliver everything we need to know about the world around us. In classical Ayurveda, the mind is considered a sense, which may also perceive "other worldly" knowledge. The senses shape our life experience.

Visualize a computer screen vs. gazing over a moonlit lake with countless stars above. If you had a choice, which would you look at? Now, think about how you felt when you walked into your grandma's house and it was filled with the scent of cookies in the oven or fresh baked bread. Now, think about how decadent a great massage feels. Recently, a dear friend of mine told me a story about a meal that was SO amazing she cried at the dinner table. Daily, we receive thousands of sensory experiences which is how we receive all our information.

DOSHAS AND THE SENSES

The doshas and senses connect our entire self to the physical world. The information received will either balance or imbalance us. Overuse, underuse, or misuse of the senses can create imbalance. An example of overuse is if we stand next to a speaker at a concert for 2 hours — our ears might ring the next day. An example of underuse is if we have a stuffed up nose and can't smell a darn thing (feels like it clogs our brain too, doesn't it?). If it's chronic, prana cannot flow to the mind. An example of misuse is watching violent or horrific movies or tv shows.

Because the senses have such a strong influence over us, we use the five senses to heal. We have to go back to where the imbalance began in order to correct it. Let's walk through a few examples of how we might be changed by information from the senses.

Let's say someone used harsh words and broke our heart. Even though it was simply a sound received by our ears, our bodies might physically hurt in our bodies (chest or stomach). The reception and digestion of those words have now made their way into our cells and changed us.

To balance our broken heart, we might need to do some internal work like journaling, talking to friends, and looking inside to see if there is a grain of truth to the words. We cannot erase the words but we can question our own behavior. We can choose to learn a lesson on forgiveness or embrace wisdom we did not have before. If we never take the time to address and cleanse those words, the imbalance will stay with us and we will stay changed.

Another example might be through taste. Let's say a person has eaten too many desserts and chocolates over the holiday season and gained 8lbs. Oopsie. The physical pounds came on through the sense of taste. We can taste a lot of flavors without eating a lot of food, however when the taste is so good, we can overdo it and end up with physical weight gain. Receiving too much taste will changed us.

To balance, we might take special care in reducing or eliminating our sugar intake for a period of time as well as focus on eating a whole foods like fruits, vegetables, healthy grains and fats and a good amount of water. We will also need to move our bodies more to digest the extra food, melt any ama, and break down low quality, excess tissues.

I'm sure you can relate to one or both of those examples so now that you have an idea of how powerful the senses are to our well being, let's walk through them one by one.

HEAR

The ears are one of the places vata sits in the body. Ears are holey, airy, spacey and their job is to bounce sound around so we can hear. Ears are sensitive and vatas will pick up on subtle sounds that the other doshas might not. Vatas are highly attuned to music and highly irritated by talk radio!

Have you ever lived or worked where there was construction going on upstairs or across the street? Madness! How about a police siren that blows by or an upstairs neighbor tap dancing on your ceiling? We can physically feel the imbalance — our shoulders might tighten up or we suddenly are unable to concentrate. We might even get angry.

On the flip side, how do you feel when you hear a gospel or children's choir? What about the jingle of your dog's collar when they are walking through the house? What about hearing a crash of ocean waves or your best friend's voice on the phone? Ahh, now these sounds might make you feel nourished, light-hearted and happy.

Not only do our ears provide information through sound, but the sounds strongly influence how we feel. If we know what sounds are most pleasurable, we can add more of those and stay away from the sounds that offend. Try to avoids sounds that rub you the wrong way — either don't listen or, find some quiet and peace as soon as you can. Re-correct by using some of your favorite sounds as a therapy technique.

ayur-tip

Cover ears in the wind! Keeping ears warm will control vata fast and warm the whole body. Vata will easily aggravate with too much wind in the ears which could cause infections, ear pain and other vata-related problems.

Sounds that are good for us:

- Chanting/mantras
- Crickets
- Classical music or "chill music"
- Wind chimes
- A fountain or waterfall
- Tree leaves and branches blowing in the wind
- Ocean waves
- Rain

Other things for the ears:

- Don't stick anything into your ear canal!
- Rub essential oils with aromatherapy on the ear lobes or anywhere above the chest
- Keep ears covered in the wind and cold
- Wear ear plugs at concerts to keep ears protected and vata pacified
- Don't listen to any music (conversations, sounds, etc.) that is not pleasing to you

LIFE CHECK HEAR

What are the things you hear daily?

_____
_____
_____

Do you over use your sense of hearing? How?

_____
_____
_____

Do you under use your sense of hearing? How?

_____
_____
_____

Are there any changes you need to make to improve the quality of how or what you hear?

_____
_____
_____

What are your favorite sounds? List and use as a therapy tool.

_____
_____
_____
_____
_____
_____
_____
_____

MY BODY IS METABOLIZING EVERYTHING I SEE, HEAR, SMELL, TASTE AND TOUCH AND TURNING IT INTO, ME.

– Deepak Chopra, *Quantum Healing*

SEE

The eyes are governed by pitta which relates to fire and light. We see colors, movement, pretty things and ugly things. When our eyes are focused, our mind is focused. Wandering eyes, triggers the mind and creates additional tasks for us. I've been guilty — too many times during my yoga practice I've stopped to sweep up dust bunnies from under the couch.

When our eyes are red or agitated it is usually because there is too much stress from intense light. Maybe our eyes get sticky and a little bloodshot at the end of the work day when we're done computering? Ever notice when we're out in the sun all day our eyes can get itchy and red too? It's all related to heat.

While we all realize how important our eyes are, we might not be aware of how we feel based on what we see. If your living room window looked over the neighbors backyard and it was full of junk like an old row boat, a trashy broken bike, strewn garbage and a blow up swimming pool with moldy water in it, would it bug you? Would you want to look out that window? In contrast, what if your living room looked over the San Francisco Bay with sparkley water, a bridge, mountains and twinkly lights at night from houses in the hills? Would you want to look out that window? For sure! You might leave the window open to catch the view all the time! It fills your experience with beauty, which influences your entire day.

When we live in a beautiful place — with our favorite photographs on display and fresh flowers on the table — we feel good, because it looks nice! If we live in clutter or darkness, we might feel uneasy or depressed because it looks like crud. And then we feel like crud. Our eyes absorb the world and are literally responsible for how we "see" the world! Whatever is in our sight line affects our bodies and spirits, so it is important to keep our eyes happy.

Keeping our eyes happy:

- Take hourly breaks from computer. Focus your gaze on trees, the sky or a distant object in nature for 1–3 minutes.
- Gaze at a candle or fireplace (three feet away)
- Rub ghee or sesame oil on bottoms of feet (feet are the action organ for the eyes)
- Do "eyeball" exercises in the a.m. Roll eyes clockwise: repeat 10x. And counterclockwise: repeat 10x
- Take out contact lenses at night!
- Wear an eye mask if there are bright lights at night
- Keep yourself beautifully organized, with only your favorite things and stay free of clutter
- Turn off all electronic screens at least one hour before bed

When we fill our eyes with natural beauty, our mind will follow suit. The mind will remain organized and peaceful with focused intention.

LIFE CHECK SEE

What are the things you see daily?

_____

_____

_____

_____

Do you over use your sense of sight? How?

_____

_____

_____

Do you under use your sense of sight? How?

_____

_____

_____

Are there any changes you need to make to improve the quality of how or what you see?

_____

_____

_____

What are your favorite sights? List and use as a therapy tool.

_____

_____

_____

_____

_____

ayur-tip

Treat your feet! Feet are the action organ for the eyes. To soothe the eyes, soothe your feet! Some ideas:

• walk on cool grass, barefoot

• enjoy a soothing foot rub

• soak feet in cool lavender-scented water

• rub sesame oil on the bottoms of your feet

• spritz feet with rose water

TOUCH

Touch balances vata and the heart chakra, which is why massage is the most nourishing therapy in Ayurveda. In fact, Ayurveda performs not two, but four-handed massages to give the grandest massages in all the land!

Skin is our largest organ. It is our buffer, receptor, and holds our insides in (thank you, skin)! Whatever touches our skin, touches our heart which sends a signal (good or bad) to our entire being. When babies cry, we pick them up, hold them, rock them so that they feel safe and comforted. Maybe we forget that adults need the same thing! Have you ever hugged someone and they say, "Oh, I needed that!" Or, have you ever given a hug to someone who's having a rough time and they begin to cry? It's because we've touched their hearts. We may not notice how lacking we are in touch until we get an unexpected hug.

No wonder we spend good money for an hour or even better, a 90-minute massage. And doesn't the time seem to fly? Massage is decadent for us because our skin is rarely pampered like that. But in Ayurveda, massage is part of the daily routine even if it's a self-massage (abhyanga p. 200).

Other than feeling nice, massage serves a physical purpose, too. We have nifty energetic freeways called srotas *(SROE-tuhz)*, which are channels running through our bodies from head to toe. Through massage, we restore proper flow through some of the srotas, which affects ALL mind, body and soul. If there is slow flow, blocked flow or flow gone haywire, we will feel it — improper flow is a source of dis-ease.

When we want to sincerely connect with people, remember the sense of touch (when appropriate and don't get in trouble with HR). If your friend is sharing a personal struggle, maybe offer your hand across the table so they feel your empathy. A good "pat on the back" let's someone know you are proud of them. A little rub on the upper back helps to relieve tension and conveys support for the other. A BIG squeeze might say more than any words ever could. There are tons of ways you can lightly convey your feelings, thoughts and emotions through touch. Be creative and sincere.

A super simple healing therapy is to give more hugs to those you care about. Hugs don't cost anything and a hug can change yours or someone else's entire mood for the day. Remember, through touch we directly connect to someone else's heart energy. So give hugs freely and often to open the hearts of those you care about.

LIFE CHECK TOUCH

What are the things you touch daily? Are they artificial or alive/natural?

_____

_____

_____

_____

Do you over use your sense of touch? How?

_____

_____

_____

Do you under use your sense of touch? How?

_____

_____

_____

Are there any changes you need to make to improve the quality of how and what you touch?

_____

_____

_____

What are your favorite things to touch? List and use as a therapy tool.

_____

_____

_____

_____

_____

_____

_____

ayur-tip

Hugs should be reserved for those you love. Hugging random people or people outside of a certain comfort zone can be a subconscious cause of stress.

wisdom

When you hug, hug over left shoulders so your hearts match up. Our tendency is to go to the right, but try the left and feel a deeper connection!

TASTE

When we eat, our mouth waters. Watery saliva is actually kapha rushing in to start the digestion process. As soon as we take a bite, what we taste sends a message to the body, giving it a heads up about what to do with that specific food. If food is tasteless, we won't digest it well. Conversely, if food is overly tasty we will likely overeat.

If we begin to think of taste as an actual therapy, we might make different food choices. We have the opportunity to use taste therapy three times a day, either balancing or imbalancing our bodies and minds. Whether we use it right or wrong will determine how our body responds and replenishes itself (or not). If we really take the time to taste our food, chew it well, slow down to eat, and eat with people we love, we will fully experience the act of eating. Taste is what enriches our eating experience. The full scoop on eating and taste is coming up in chapters 7–9.

A Tasteful Question: What does Ayurveda say about chewing gum?

Chewing gum is something we may overlook because, well, gum is tiny. And we don't swallow it — at least we aren't supposed to. It's kind of like nothing. So why would we consider chewing gum as any sort of influential factor in staying balanced? Because in Ayurveda, everything counts!

The answer is that chewing gum is vata increasing and disturbs agni. Sorry for the news. It's kind of like fidgeting (also vata) except with our mouth. It's constant motion, constant action and it's rather subconscious because we do it without really paying attention. Any mindless action (especially for those gum snappers!) can increase vata since vata is action/motion. Because digestion starts in the mouth with salivation, we are jump starting that process over and over as well as swallowing lots of air. So, the verdict on gum? It increases vata. If you have any digestive issues, try avoiding gum. Even though it is wee tiny, the smallest things can make the biggest difference.

LIFE CHECK TASTE

How might you over use or wrongly use your sense of taste?
Hint: Are foods you eat artificial or natural?

_____

_____

_____

_____

Is your sense of taste underused? How?

_____

_____

_____

_____

Are there any changes you need to make to improve the quality of what you taste or how you use your sense of taste?

_____

_____

_____

_____

What are your favorite tastes? Do they balance or imbalance your dosha?

_____

_____

_____

_____

List balancing tastes/foods for you and use as a therapy tool.

_____

_____

_____

_____

SMELL

Smell is governed by kapha as it relates to the earth element. It is said in the Westie world that our sense of smell is the sense closest linked to memory (kaphas never forget, just like elephants!). Maybe the smell of dewy grass and mud brings you back to warm summer nights as a kid. The smell of "spring mist" plug-in air freshener reminds your of college dorm life. The smell of baby lotion makes your heart ache a teensy bit because your child is no longer a baby. Maybe the reason we get transported so quickly is because our nose acts as a direct link to our mind. Whatever comes in through the nose instantly influences the mind and from there, the mind controls the rest of us.

This is why aromatherapy (and pranayama) is an effective therapy for emotional imbalance. When used specifically with the doshas in mind, natural scents can trigger different emotions. As with anything else, not all smells benefit all doshas. Rather, each scent has doshas and elements to them, so we have to use the right ones for our individuality.

GROUNDING SCENTS FOR VATA: LAVENDER, JASMINE, PATCHOULI, FRANKINSENSE, GERANIUM

SOOTHING SCENTS FOR PITTA: ROSE, CHAMOMILE, CUCUMBER, LAVENDER, MINT

INVIGORATING SCENTS FOR KAPHA: GRAPEFRUIT, YLANG YLANG, EUCALYPTUS, GERANIUM, LEMON

LIFE CHECK SMELL

What are the things you smell daily? Are they artificial or natural?

_____

_____

_____

Do you over use or wrongly use your sense of smell? How?

_____

_____

_____

Is your sense of smell underused? How?

_____

_____

_____

Are there any changes you need to make to improve the quality of what you smell?

_____

_____

_____

What are your favorite smells? Write an emotion next to each smell.
List and use as a therapy tool.

_____

_____

_____

_____

_____

_____

SENSORY BALANCING FOR THE DOSHAS

Vata is balanced by touch and sound. Warm oil massage, soft fabrics (hello, fleece!), big warm hugs from loved ones, calming music, peaceful sounds in nature, mantras, are all ways to calm vata down.

Robotic or stiff touches, cold air or foods, scratchy fabrics, aggressive or loud music, talk radio, construction noise, sirens, smoke detector and beeping trucks, will send a vata up the walls.

Pitta is balanced by sight. Keeping it neat, organized, clean, feng shui'ed, and well presented, will calm a pitta because they can finally relax. If pitta notices visual disarray, they cannot rest or concentrate until they tidy up.

Clutter, disorganization, shower mildew, dust bunnies, spelling errors and Excel files that "could have been organized better" will send pitta into hyper-organization and cleaning mode. They will take it all on themselves to control it and fix it.

Kapha is balanced by taste and smell. Delicious food, a large variety of tastes and spices, the smell of garlic, barbecue, candles, scent sticks, flowers, gardening and fireplaces all make kaphas feel alive.

Goopy, heavy, bland, wet foods will offend a kapha. They usually do not like mayonnaise or thick oatmeal. If smells are too smoky, musky, heavy or earthy, kapha will feel stifled instead of light, fresh, airy and invigorated.

truth

Only natural smells are beneficial for healing. Artificial smells have no natural intelligence and therefore will imbalance the doshas over time. So put down the Glade® and reach for aromatherapy oils and a diffuser instead.

insight

When I smell Jamba Juice,® it reminds me of being jobless when I first moved to San Francisco. I used to sit on a bench outside of Jamba Juice with my laptop to get free wi-fi while I looked frantically online for a job. To this day when I smell Jamba Juice, I get a slightly anxious stomach ache because the smell transports me back to that space and time of stress. Smell directly links to our memories and past experiences.

challenge

Do a "screen fast" for five days and don't use screens after work hours. Reflect on how you feel and what else you were able to do when not hooked in to your screens.

I SCREEN, YOU SCREEN

Most of us spend our days on computer screens and smart phones, only to come home and spend more time on screens at night. Email, online shopping, blogging, gaming, TV-ing and Facebooking are just a few examples of how these screens can sneak into our worlds after hours and suck up our time! The thing about screens is that they are not alive. They don't have prana. They make us feel tired rather than energized. We might even feel like we have "no time" because time seems to vanish into the abyss of the screen and before we know it, it's way past bedtime.

Friends, screens are vata increasing. They can cause sleep problems, depression, anxiety, evoke a sense of loneliness and low self-worth. And, of course, cause eye problems (pitta) as well as kapha aggravation because of sedentary habits. We need a break from these things, so unplug each night at least an hour before bedtime.

Screens have their purpose, but they absolutely should not to trump exercise, healthy eating, good sleep, fun hobbies, and time with family. Those are LIFE! Screens are not. So, while we rely on screens to get our work done and sometimes watch an inspiring TV show, I encourage you to put down the screen once in a while or even take a screen detox of 3–5 days.

LIFE CHECK SO MANY SCREENS!

How much time a day do you spend on the computer including work, emails, shopping, Facebook, etc.?

_____

_____

How much time a day do you spend on your smart phone?

_____

_____

Make a list of all the things you could do if you didn't spend your evenings on screens.

_____

_____

_____

_____

_____

_____

_____

_____

_____

_____

_____

_____

_____

_____

Look at all those things!

As you've learned, the senses connect our physical body to experiences and bring an abundant variety of information to us. As we have spent most of our time on the physical body, let us shift over to the mind. Unlike the senses, the mind pervades our entire being and it is not connected to the physical body solely, it also connects to the spirit.

12
MIND-FULL

The control center: our mind

learn

Our sense organs have their limits. Ears can only hear. Eyes can only see. The mind, however, is limitless. It works with our sense organs but can also fly solo, functioning without them as we sleep or meditate. The mind is not restricted to a small part of the body, the mind pervades our entirety.

Our mind can only attach to one sense at a time. When we multitask, our mind goes all over the place which creates mental and physical agitation.

Our physical posture also controls our mental attitude. Proper positioning helps develop a devotional mood and slows down restlessness.

The mind receives vibrations from the sense organs for decisions.

OUR DECISIONS

If we want to change our body, we must first change our mind. Our bodies don't go around doing things on their own, they need a control center to tell them what to do. The mind is that decision-making control center and our body follows suit. If we don't have a healthy mind, there's no way we will have a healthy body and this is why the mind-body connection is vital. They rely on each other to keep the self whole and thriving.

The mind does not have one location (it is not the same as the brain). It flows everywhere. We feel it mostly in the heart and chest between the lungs. There are subtle channels that emerge from those sources which circulate prana throughout the body. When these subtle channels are blocked or flow in the wrong direction, it causes psychological problems.

If we want to change our body, we must first change our mind.

Remember, mistaken intellect or making wrong choices can be anything we do that we already know is not good for us. We can all relate to that experience. How many times have you heard people say, "I have to exercise more." "I need to eat better." "I need to quit smoking." "I wish I didn't spend so much money." Right? We give ourselves all kinds of "shoulds" to try and keep ourselves healthy, but maybe it doesn't come to fruition on the other end. The good news? ALL of these habits can be controlled by our choices and our mind controls our bodies.

Here, let's talk about drinking alcohol as an example.

After one drink, we feel a little relaxed as our muscles release and our mind gets more dull. Since we like our mellow mood, we have another drink. After the second drink, our buddhi or "right" mind might say, "Warning! If you have a third drink you will spend way too much money on drinks *and* you will be hungover *and* totally useless tomorrow! Don't do it." But since we are not in our "right" mind we tell buddhi to sit down and as our better judgment gets quiet, we choose to have a third drink. And after the third drink, we let our hair down and have a fortthh drink. After the fourth drink we really have no mind left so we have a a fiffffffthhh and then sixxcchhttthh drink, and a whole ton of bad choices could ensue after this. Chowin' pepperoni pizza at 2 a.m., a lost wallet in a cab, you said something mean to your friend, you fell and hit your face, etc., Yah? All this dumb stuff! It's a perfect example of how our mind has been fed the wrong thing and we can no longer make the right choices. This happens a lot, you guys!

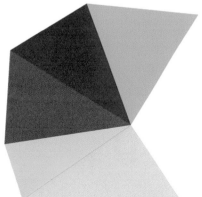

To illustrate my point, that was a totally non-Ayurvedic example but, man, I bet you could tell me at least five friends that have pulled shenanigans like that. Our mind is powerful! But when we lose our mind, we lose our judgement, our right action, and our wisdom. So when our mind guides us to do the right thing, our body needs to put the practice in motion. Yes, even if we are too tired or are uninspired or whatever excuses our body is throwing at us. From this moment forward, start listening and moving according to what the our healthy, wise mind says!

THE MIND DOES NOT HAVE ONE LOCATION IT PERVADES THE ENTIRE BODY

insight

Sattva does not cause disease, but rajas and tamas definitely can. Too much sattva is not really possible, although I suppose we could just walk around in a blissy state and not achieve any of our goals. Just like the doshas, we need all three tri-gunas but the two that will imbalance us are rajas and tamas.

learn

Microwaves alter the quality of our food. Use real heat/fire as much as you can.

Tamas is what helps us sleep. We need darkness just as we need the light.

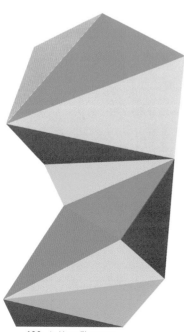

To keep our minds good n' healthy, we can start with the quality of our food. What we put in our bodies will feed our mind too, so "food" should be high quality in order to keep the mind high quality. Remember, just like the doshas have qualities, foods have qualities too. And, based on the qualities of the foods, they will give qualities to the mind.

Too much or over-processed sugar gives us a racing mind; too much spicy and salty food give us an aggressive mind; veggies and fruits give us a "clean" mind; milk soothes our mind.

The tastes are not just for the body alone. The tastes also influence the mind and our emotions, too (it's all connected). The **trigunas** are where the connection of food, physical body and mind all hold hands in a kumbayah.

The Trigunas

SATTVA – PURITY, HARMONY
RAJAS – ACTION, CHANGE
TAMAS – INERTIA, DARKNESS

TRIGUNAS

There are three qualities of the mind or, trigunas (tri-GOON-uhs). As you remember, "guna" means quality, so we can think of them as energies, qualities or states of mind. The trigunas are sattva (SAT-vuh), rajas (RAH-jus) and tamas (TOM-us) which are the three primal qualities in our consciousness (I know, this Ayurveda thing keeps getting deeper, doesn't it?).

Sattva (sattvic) is the quality that promotes purity of thought, absolute harmony, and right action. Sattva is inward focus on what the soul desires. Sattva creates peace, unconditional happiness, love and contentment. We all need more sattva!

Rajas (rajasic) is the quality responsible for creating turbulence, stimulation and transformation. It is action, dominance, power and prestige. It is attachment to the senses and desires, living through the ego. Rajas is outward focus. Rajas helps us achieve our goals, yet is attached to the outcome of our goals, which can cause suffering because we are never satisfied. Most of us live in rajas!

Tamas (tamasic) is darkness, heaviness, ignorance, close mindedness, lack of awareness, obstruction, decay. Tamas is downward focus. In the mind tamas causes fear, rage, deep depression, hatred. We might go through brief moments of tamas, but if you were a heavily tamasic person you would not be reading a book on Ayurveda.

There is a balance between the three qualities and each has their place. Among the three, rajas and tamas may lead to disease. Sattva never causes disease because it is totally pure which cannot be imbalanced. The goal is to bring more sattvic qualities into our lives. If we were solely sattvic, we would consistently adhere to right choice and right action. Even tamas has its place when something "dies," or comes to an end. Sleep is tamas because we are ignorant during that time — totally in the dark.

The goal is to bring more sattvic qualities into our lives.

If there is too much rajas quality in our mind, we might work ourselves crazy until we get what our ego thinks is "top-notch," and still may not be satisfied. So we strive some more and then end up with stress-related health problems. Too much tamas is a more severe and includes addictions, psychological problems, suicidal tendencies, hatefulness, vindictiveness and intense attachment to pleasure and material things.

The chart shows how we might react in the mental state of the tri-gunas depending on who we are. You can see that a rajasic vata will act very differently than a rajasic pitta.

QUALITIES OF MIND/TRIGUNAS

	SATTVIC	RAJASIC	TAMASIC
Vata	Creative, Inspired, Enthusiastic, Genuine Artistic, Intuitive	Nervous, Anxious, Manic, Hyper, Worrisome, Fearful	Depressed, Addicted, Psychological problems, Suicidal
Pitta	Strong Leader, Clear Thinking, Spiritual Teacher, Perceptive	Angry, Hot Tempered, Judgemental, Resentful, Controlling, Jealous	Violent, Hateful, Vindictive, Hurtful, Murderers
Kapha	Nuturing, Peaceful, Loving, Compassionate, Jolly, Generous, Forgiving	Attached to things/ objects, Stubborn, Possessive, Holds Grudges	Intensely attached to pleasure and material things, Self Loathing, Lethargic, Thieves

HOW TO BE MORE SATTVIC

- Start with nutrition! Choose food high in prana, avoiding canned, frozen, fried, fast food, refined sugars and processed foods. Remember, these foods are lifeless and give no nourishment to the mind or body.
- Surround yourself with positive and loving people
- Be practical and realistic — face the truth and accept yourself
- Volunteer, mentor, coach, donate. Give a little of what you have, to others in some way.
- Listen to your buddhi, your inner wisdom
- Do pranayama and meditation. These directly channel and nourish the mind to increase sattva.
- Avoid TV shows with highly stressful or aggressive topics

Sattva for the doshas

VATA. HAVE FAITH INSTEAD OF FEAR. TRUST AND THINK ABOUT WHEN YOU FELT GOOD, SAFE, CONFIDENT, ON CLOUD NINE.

PITTA. HAVE COMPASSION FOR OTHERS. GIVE, EMBODY HUMILITY, VOLUNTEER, TONE DOWN THE EGO.

KAPHA. THROW THINGS AWAY. PRACTICE NON-ATTACHMENT TO EMOTIONS, MEMORIES, MATERIAL THINGS

MOOD FOOD

Every morsel we put into our body has energy connected to it. Consider it the driver of our moods and intellect. It's mood food. The energy and qualities from food is what we ingest and as you know by now, is what we become. If foods we eat are made from highly processed, lifeless ingredients, our perception will be that of a lifeless world. Flip that instead to eat lively, fresh foods, and we are going to feel lively and fresh. Food should also feed all the senses. It should look good, smell good, feel good and taste good. In fact, in Indian tradition, eating with the hands (there is even a word for it: hasta pradhana tamah) is considered the best instrument for eating. It's a full experience, not just a quick jam of food in the mouth so we can carry on with our busy-ness.

So, which foods create good moods? Check out the chart below to see the breakdown of sattvic, rajasic, and tamasic foods. Overall, the best foods for us are veggies and grains! Fruits and water! Ghee from happy cows and dairy, too, if it comes from a good place. In addition to foods, make sure to drink plenty of water. Plants wither and animals throw their water dish around when it's empty. Without enough water, our mood will wither too, as a warning sign. Aren't our bodies so smart to give us warning signs? Love the bodies. Incorporating more happy foods, full of sun, nourished by water and nature will bring about happiness, joy, focus, and inner peace.

Plant-based foods. Veggies, fruits and grains are all sattvic and high in prana. Notice anything they have in common? They all come from plants! Plants are always happy, they have no emotions or stresses. Plants are certain the sun will come out, rain will give them a drink and they will grow while they reach for the stars. Pretty great, right? Wouldn't you like to be like that?

dohsa fun

Vatas are highly sensitive to moods and can swing in a positive or negative direction very quickly.

Pittas are not moody but they can get firey.

Kaphas are not moody, mostly happy.

nourish

Always buy full fat and local organic dairy when possible. When the fat is taken out the food has been altered from its natural state.

nourish

If you find you are in a rajasic or tamasic state more than you'd like to be, pay serious attention to what you are eating and start there first. Make adjustments and begin to incorporate foods closer to the source.

As you eat better foods, the mind will give you signals to make better choices. Then, act on those choices

SATTVA	RAJAS	TAMAS
Foods that promotes purity of mind, peace, intelligence and right decisions.	Foods that give motivation. Keeps us attached to the ego and creates desires.	Foods that destroy our resistance to disease. Clouds the mind. Promotes negative emotions.
MILK	COFFEE/ BLACK TEA	ALCOHOL
HERBAL TEA	CHICKEN/RED MEAT	FAST FOOD
GHEE	EGGS	FRIED FOOD
RICE	ONION	FROZEN FOOD
FRESH SWEET FRUITS	GARLIC	CANNED/STALE FOOD
FRESH VEGGIES	CITRUS FRUITS	REFINED SUGARS
HONEY	VERY SPICY FOODS	TOBACCO
NUTS	CHOCOLATE	SODA
MUNG DAHL	SALT	OVEREATING
PEACE WHILE EATING	EATING TOO FAST	

Let's be careful not to over-build our body with meat. Too much meat will create excess tissues causing weight gain and health problems as our bodies try to interpret and digest animal tissues. Our bodies are happiest with mostly plants and a small amount of meat depending on our dosha and state of agni.

Now! Let's look at the other side to include foods that are highly tamasic contain little or no life. Those include alcohol, fast foods, canned, stale, and frozen foods. The prana those foods had originally has left or has been processed-to-death.

Meats. Are animals always happy? Not necessarily. Do they live in the sun? Some do, but it's not guaranteed. Whatever life that animal lived, we eat it. If we eat animals that lived under poor conditions that created negative emotions (like fear, panic, aggression), we will become the same. If we choose to eat meat, we need to make sure our meat comes from happy, healthy animals. As a best practice, if you are unsure of the quality of the meat on your plate, don't eat it.

Ayurveda says some people need meat to keep them strong. Meat is literally the tissues of animals and once we eat it, those tissues will also become ours so meat can be very beneficial to build strength. Depending on the person, when get sick or weak (or pregnant!) and cannot build enough of our own tissues, meat can be used as a highly-effective medicine.

FEEDING YOUR MIND AND THE MIND OF OTHERS

We've said that eating while happy is the most important thing we can do for our digestion, right? Now, here is something you might not think about. Have you ever judged or commented on someone else's meal? Stuff like this: "Eu, how can you eat that? Do you know how much fat is in that? OMG those things have way too many carbs. Dairy isn't good for you, you know. Is that *all* you're eating for lunch?"

Friends, please do not comment on or judge other peoples' food, particularly when they are about to eat it. You are harming their mind and digestion. What would normally be an enjoyable meal, could spoil in an instant because of your words. Let them eat happy. Share the helpful things you know about nutrition, yes, but choose an appropriate time and manner when doing so.

Along these same lines, be mindful of what is shared on social media. Are you sharing anything that might harm others' minds? If your friends are happily browsing on Facebook only to stumble upon your image of animals being harmed or a terrible news story, how did you just affect their day? What if the stream was left open and their young child happened to see it while they walked past from the computer? Remember, our mind lives in the body, so whatever we see and hear gets processed and treated as if it's really happening. A highly intense, stressful or traumatic television show could stick in our body-minds for months, even years. We replay those events in our mind as if they really happened and our cells are recreated accordingly. There is enough stress and scary things in our real world without needing to add television shows accentuating so much bad stuff. It's too much for our minds and bodies to bear. To balance out life's real traumas, let us protect and grow our minds. Let us bring awareness knowing that through what we share, can either send a sparkle of happiness or a ding of awfulness. I'm all for the sparkles! Let us share gifts of wonder, amazement, delight, love, compassion and humor. Let us shine a light and leave the darkness behind. Let us tell stories that inspire and make us smarter. Let us cheer each other on for overcoming seemingly impossible obstacles. Let us celebrate how people succeed at doing their very best with what they have.

Your body is a temple but before the body comes the mind. Your mind is sacred. Don't poison it. Protect it. Flourish with it.

Dude, how cool would it be to have an all positive news channel? Or at least realistically highlighting awesome, inventive people. Yes! Why, it could be called, "Monica B's Best News Ever." And I would fill peoples' minds and hearts with pure gold. The stories would highlight how people work together, stories of compassion, stories of good health and how we experience simple miracles every day. Thirty minutes of that five times a week? Like nectar for our hearts! Imagine what it would do for the world! Sign me up. I didn't digress much in this book like I do on **heymonicab.com**, but there's one for ya.

MEDITATION

Phew, our minds do lots of things, don't they? Thank you, mind! Based on all the work our mind does for us, we should rest our minds daily. Raise your hands: how many of you have a regular meditation practice? Hey, that's quite a few, good job! Now, if meditation sounds too new-agey, hippie-dippie or something that feels too foreign to try, let me see if I can shed some light.

Think of the mind as a snow globe. Now *shake* the snow globe! This is the typical state of our mind, where everything is happening all at once and there is barely any clarity. Can you see what's in the snow globe or through the other side of the glass? No way, it's all stirred up and there is so much stuff — we might only see slight fragments of the full picture as we peek through the scatters. Meditation happens when the snow starts to fall and settle. Only then can actually see what's inside the globe and in our souls. When the snow settles and the globe becomes clear, that is what meditation does for our mind.

Mediation is space and clarity. In a sense, it might be considered nothing. That might be hard for people to grasp so if you have to grasp something, then think about meditation as focusing on the breath. It is the absence of

tip
Hey, so, I cannot watch much TV at all because if I did I would have nightmares. It's OK if you are the same way, you don't have to watch or listen to anything that might make a dent in your harmonious mind. Remember this for your children too. Protect their innocent minds for as long as you can and fill them with only the very best.

resource
Have you heard of The Laughter Guru? Or, Laughter Yoga? **laughteryoga.org**

thought and simply, pure awareness. Awareness is the first step in healing and into observing the desire of our soul.

> ### I am soul. If I don't know who I am, I will always be irritated.

If we live separate from our soul (or spirit), we feel uncomfortable, mis-aligned and agitated while finding fulfillment and purpose will seem difficult. We often search externally, flipping over rock after rock to fulfill our desires, but the trick is that the fulfillment comes from inside. We have everything we need, but if we do not spend time with our insides and are unaware of our soul, we will always feel lost. We want to live better by practicing Ayurveda with eternal practices like a customized diet, the daily routine and exercise while we pay close attention to doshas, but we will only get partial benefits if we don't include meditation. We talked about the body, the mind, and now, the spirit. All three go together, none without the other.

Let's round out this wonderful Ayurvedic knowledge you've been absorbing by including peace of mind, in order to reach the spirit. Even five minutes a day does wonders, so if that's all you can do at first, then that's great.

How to meditate:

1) You may choose to set a timer for 5–10 minutes. If you do, make sure it's a pleasant "wake up" sound like gentle bells, chimes or harp.
2) Sit with chakras aligned, feet on the floor. Or, lay on your back in savasana (arms next to you palms up, feet hip width apart and let them flop).
3) Take 5–10 deep and slow inhales and exhales, breathing from your lower belly not the chest.
4) Let your breath return to normal and observe the ins and outs…until the timer goes off.

Sometimes "not having thoughts" is the hardest thing not to think about! Don't worry, if you have thoughts let them show up and then just bring your attention back to your breath. Same thing with external noises, "Hello, noises. Hello, breath." You can choose to put on some light music if you choose. Guided meditations are great too.

Overall, remember, you are all you need. We are fully equipped with intelligence, brilliance, love, talent, creativity — it's all inside! We just need to give ourselves space so we begin to understand how our soul wants to shine.

13
OM-THERAPIES

Who doesn't need a little therapy?

There are many therapies in Ayurveda, most of which require proper training because they will need to be tweaked for each person. Let's walk through some simple and safe at-home therapies, as well as some therapies you may hear about that require the guidance of an Ayurvedic practitioner. I will highlight the difference so you don't go willy nilly putting oil in places, making potions and making yourself sick. OK?

Each therapy works on a different part of the body but has a myriad of influence. While the therapy is localized, the effects are widespread across body, mind, and spirit. For example, massage is localized on the skin, but the benefits go far beyond the skin. Abhyanga is calming for the mind providing clarity and focus, releases muscle tension, promotes sound sleep, tones our deepest tissues and helps open channels. So we might as well start with abhyanga!

Do-it-yourself therapies

ABHYANGA

A warm oil massage, or abhyanga (ah-bee-YOUNG-guh), is probably the most well-known therapy in Ayurveda. Abhyanga benefits all three doshas, so you'll need to use the right oil and the right pressure for your dosha because even massage is customized. If abhyanga is administered the wrong way, it could do more harm than good.

Vata abhyanga. Vatas need a gentle warm massage to ground, nourish and put them at ease. Vatas are thin-skinned and kinda boney, so too much pressure or vigor can cause them pain and discomfort, which is the opposite of ease! A wrong massage could easily imbalance a vata. No bueno. Long gentle strokes is what vata needs. They will feel relaxed, strong and nourished — they will sleep like a baby. The best oils to use are sesame (which is warming) or almond oil. The amount of oil for vatas will be more generous because their dry little selves will soak it up like a sponge. They need it. All oils should be warmed before putting on vata skin for easy absorption and because warmth has direct skin contact, bringing instant tranquility.

Pitta abhyanga. Pittas need a massage with precision and good pressure. If their muscles haven't been "worked" they won't be satisfied and then their mind will be focus on how unsatisfied they are. Pittas build their muscles easily and have moderately thick skin so they can tolerate more pressure and need extra attention on releasing and relaxing their muscle tissue. While they like good pressure, if it hurts, they'll get pissed. Be firm and precise but don't hurt them. The best oils for pittas are coconut or almond oil.

learn

Health and disease have two locations — the physical body and the mind. Both locations have to be addressed or the disease will not be cured completely.

ayur-tip

If you THINK you are going to get sick, you probably will. Keep your mind clear and think healthy. When doing pranayama, inhale pure life and healing energy. On the exhale, release toxins, negative energy and negative thoughts. Let it all go. Pure mind equals a pure body. And as usual, wash your hands a lot, don't lick shopping carts and don't let people cough on you. And, if you feel you are about to be sick, REST.

"The body of one who uses oil massage regularly does not become affected much even if subjected to injury or strenuous work. By using oil massage daily, a person is endowed with pleasant touch, trimmed body parts and becomes strong, charming and least affected by old age."
Charaka Samhita, Vol. 1, V: 88-89

Kapha abhyanga. Kaphas need a very different massage experience. Kaphas will like any massage they are given, but actually need a vigorous and dry massage. Take a moment and rub your hands together *fast!* Feel that heat? Dry, heat, and motion all balance kapha. That friction is what kaphas need for their massage because vigorous massage breaks up heavy, stagnant muscle and fat tissues to bring more fluidity, warmth and lightness.

In traditional Ayurveda, kapha massage is practiced with a dry mixture of chick pea power and some herbs in a poultice (or loose). Instead of hands, the poultices are used directly on the skin in synchronized, and somewhat forceful motion. Now, it's not exactly relaxing but kaphas don't need relaxation (they have that naturally), they need invigoration. Kaphas, you do not have to use a dry chick pea powder for massage — leave that to the professionals — but the oil should be light like sunflower oil and the massage should be fast. Kaphas can handle firm pressure.

Notice how different each of these massages are? A vata would die (not literally) from a kapha-type massage and a pitta would not stand for it! Kaphas and vatas would not enjoy someone digging in to their muscles. Pittas would get irritated if their massage felt more like a tickle or if their sensitive skin was roughed up with gritty warm powder. Kaphas will benefit from more strokes and good pressure. Pittas focus on the muscles. Vatas focus on the skin. Now that you understand the different styles, let's do the massage!

How to do abhyanga:

1) Choose the warm oil best for your dosha.
2) Stand on a towel you don't care about.
3) Using your dosha "type" as the guide for the pressure and speed, apply the oil starting from toe to head. We want absorption, not an oil slick, but no tugging on the skin. Start with your feet and legs. Use long strokes on the bones with some pressure up toward the heart, then go back down with less pressure, then back UP toward the heart. Make clockwise circles around the joints and clockwise circles around the belly button with some pressure. Don't forget your booty. Reach your back the best you can, upward toward the shoulders. Long strokes on arms up and toward the heart/shoulders. Get hands starting from the base and clockwise again around joints. Strokes go upwards on the neck and face.
4) Sit and do some nadi shodhanam (p. 167) for 10 minutes.
5) Get in a warm (not scalding) shower and wash off the oil.
6) Get out and dab yourself off. The oil will be absorbed into your skin, leaving it super soft!
7) Enjoy your baby-soft skin, relaxed muscles and happy mind.

---

how to warm your oil

Put oil in a small squeezy plastic bottle. Put water in a pot on the stove and float squeezy bottle in the water to warm it. Takes 5–10 minutes. Test. If it's too hot, add more room-temp oil.

---

ayur-tip

Warm your oil while you brush your teeth and scrape your tongue.

---

what you'll need for massage

- 1 plastic squeeze bottle filled with your oil
- 1 pot of hot water (float your squeeze bottle in there to warm the oil)
- 1 towel you don't care about
- 10+ minutes

Benefits of abhyanga

- Produces softness, strength and color to the body
- Decreases the effects of aging
- Bestows good vision
- Nourishes the body
- Increases longevity
- Benefits sleep patterns
- Benefits skin
- Strengthens the body's tolerance
- Imparts a firmness to the limbs
- Gives tone and vigor to the dhatus (tissues) of the body
- Stimulates the internal organs of the body, including circulation
- Pacifies vata and pitta and harmonizes kapha

Benefits of applying oil to the scalp

- Makes hair grow luxuriantly, thick, soft and glossy
- Soothes and invigorates the sense organs
- Lessens (even removes!) facial wrinkles

TONGUE SCRAPING

Salivating is the first step in digestion, which pools in to our mouths beginning the digestive/breakdown process. Knowing digestion starts in our mouth, this scraping-the-tongue thing will make more sense, hopefully.

When we wake in the morning we have night time gunk on our tongue. The night tongue gunk is not necessarily ama, but it is a bit of coating. We want to want to scrape the tongue seven times to remove this layer of coating. Then we can brush our teeth and rinse our mouth.

Benefits of scraping the tongue:

- Cleans the tongue so we can taste food better and therefore digest better
- Stimulates digestion
- Tells us if ama is there
- Prevents bacteria from getting ingested

ayur-tip

You wouldn't put water on your skin if it's dry, right? No, because your skin would only get drier. Yet in most lotions, the first ingredient is water, followed closely by alcohol! Bah! Your plan to moisturize is instantly foiled. The skin eats (it's an organ, after all), and anything on the skin is absorbed by the body. A general rule is, if we can't eat it, it should not go on our skin. We can eat oils!

MINI AT-HOME KITCHARI CLEANSE

A kitchari (KIT-cha-ree) cleanse is a mono diet to nourish and reset the digestive system. Simply commit to 3–7 days for the cleanse. How do you know if you "need" it? If you feel emotionally depressed, physically heavy, have any symptoms of ama, or are just not feeling like yourself, a kitchari cleanse will do you a world of good. You know yourself better than anyone else, so you be the judge of when you need it. This can be done any time.

What is kitchari? Kitchari is a traditional Indian dish made of digestive spices, basmati rice, mung dahl and veggies of your choice. It's a staple in Indian households to accompany many dishes. If a food could wrap you in a cozy blanket, it would be kitchari.

Kitchari is tri-doshic, sattvic and wonderfully easy to digest. It is also a great source of protein because the mung dal is a complete food and is excellent for detoxification and de-aging of cells as it nourishes all the tissues of the body. It is the go-to Ayurvedic fix when our mind, body, and/or emotions need to hit the reset button. Because of its purity, negative emotions lighten and dissipate. We may find that digestive heaviness, bloating, indigestion and constipation will go away. Cloudiness of mind, confusion, uncertainty, or indecisiveness will open to clarity.

The combination of spices work directly on agni and the digestive tract, which helps gather and expel any old, unneeded, unwanted food stuffs. It also helps burn off ama — yay! It will create a peaceful mind as well (all connected, remember? Anything backed up in the guts will back up the mind too). The ingredients in kitchari are sattvic so a few days of eating this pure food will turn your mind easy, peaceful, and clear. If you likey the sound of kitchari so far, let's go into more cleanse detail.

How to do the cleanse:

- In the morning, while sipping ginger tea, make a nice batch of kitchari (recipe p. 154) with peaceful music on.
- Have kitchari for breakfast, lunch and dinner. **Note:** If your tongue is pink, drizzle ghee on top. If your tongue is not pink, wait to add extra ghee until your tongue is pink.
- If you are not hungry, sip ginger tea and/or warm water (can add lemon only if you are vata and don't have ama) until you feel hungry. **Note:** You might poop before you feel hungry which is normal.
- Sip herbal teas or water between meals.

food

Ajwain and hing are both anti-flatulent and are used often in lentil dishes. Eliminates the toots!

Kitchari is meant to be a mild food, so that it resets our taste buds. Overly salty, spicy or falsely tasty foods kick our taste buds into overdrive, which make us crave and eat more. After the cleanse, food will taste extra good and we will be satisfied with less in quantity.

tip

If we are constipated, we will not feel hungry. If we pay attention, we will notice that we are hungry after we poop!

Vatas and pittas should have a nice amount of ghee with their kitchari. Kaphas should have none or just a little.

Kitchari for vatas should be made with more water so the consistency is more wet and sticky. Kitchari for kaphas should be made with less water and therefore, more dry.

- If you are very hungry between meals, have a piece of fruit like banana, peeled apple or pear with tea.
- Do this for 3–7 days.
- Optional: Keep a daily journal how you feel along the way.

After the cleanse is just as important as the cleanse itself.

It is important to slowly rebuild agni to be good and strong. Don't say, "Yay! My cleanse is over! I'm going out for steak and wine and chocolate cake!" No, no, no, don't do that. If you eat normally right after the cleanse, agni won't be strong enough, and you will start building up ama right away. Counterproductive!

Instead build the digestive system back up slowly. The day after the cleanse, have liquid soup with veggies. The next day, have soup with veggies and rice or noodles, maybe a slice of bread. Next day you can start eating normally. See that? A little step-by-step process to eating normal again. **Note:** You must do this with ANY cleanse or you will reverse the benefits and actually make your digestion worse. It's really important!

Now you have a stockpile of safe at-home therapies. And you probably want to scoot off and try a few (I know you). Go for it! There are also times when you need the guidance of a trained Ayurvedic practitioner who, as we discussed, can adjust therapies to your unique self. We are going to explore those next. **Remember:** Don't try them at home…at least not until your practitioner personally teaches you how and says it's OK.

ayur-tip

A simple kitchari cleanse is kind of like an tune-up. It is regular maintenance that makes a big difference over a lifetime.

what's with the oils?

Used inside and out in Ayurveda, oils are an essential ingredient to keep the body nourished, rejuvenated, toned calm and supple. Oil soaks into the skin and reaches all our bodily tissues even on the deepest level.

We might think that the best way to moisturize is to drink a lot of water but water doesn't necessarily "moisturize." Sometimes it just runs right through. Oil is unctuous which works to soften our outsides and gets deep in our tissues to keep our emotional, mental and physical bodies balanced.

WAYS YOU CAN USE VARIOUS OILS

Almond Oil. Good for vata and pitta externally. Light enough to use before bed near the eyes to reduce crows feet. Great for full body massage and will not irritate pitta's sensitive skin.

Coconut Oil. Good for pitta internally and externally. Has a cooling effect on the inside and outside of the body. Will solidify at room temperature so you may have to scoop it out and warm it up.

Flaxseed Oil. Good for internal oleation and helps with constipation if you are ghee shy. Don't heat it. Drizzle on veggies and rice bowls.

Ghee. Eat it. Melt on pastas, bread, oatmeal, mashed potatoes, veggies, baked apples. Increases agni (digestive fire), reduces vata and pitta, nourishes all tissues, relieves constipation, and stabilizes moods. **Note:** Make sure you don't over do it. Too much ghee can quickly and easily cause ama.

Olive Oil. Not talked about in classical Ayurveda because Indians don't have olive trees…but I've used it on my hands and face for a little extra elasticity and softening. And obviously for cooking, dipping, drizzling on foods.

Sesame Oil. Use internal and external. Great for abhyanga (vata) and karnapurana. Use "cold-pressed" for external, not the "toasted" kind or you'll smell like Asian food.

Therapies - expert required

There are approximately 2 billion (I might have exaggerated just then) combinations of therapies. We may practice shirodhara on the client, which is a warm oil-drizzle on the forehead. We may also practice heat therapy like steam or dry heat to make the client sweat. Each therapy is totally customized to the person, so while it's not possible to list everything, just know that some of these therapies are highly comprehensive and individualized.

KARNAPURANA

Karnapurana (karna-POOr-nuh) means, filling the ears with warm oil. Karnapurana is a therapy that should be done under a practitioner's care. Vatas especially benefit because the warming oil goes directly into one of the seats of vata, our ears.

Potential benefits of karnapurana:

- Relieves insomnia
- Relieves ringing in the ears
- Eliminates headaches
- Relieves TMJ or tension in the jaw
- Calms anxiety, panic, or chronic worrying
- Reduces effect of jet-lag
- Eliminates ears popping/crackling in high altitude

Other benefits may include:

- Improves hearing
- Strengthens the bones in the ear
- Prevents neck stiffness
- Loosens ear wax (who doesn't want that?!)

NASYA

Nasya (NAHs-yuh) is putting oil drops or powder in the nose. Surprise, surprise, more oil. You'd think this was an Ayurvedic book or something. It is important that our beloved passageways stay nourished and clean so prana can flow through properly. Nasya feels a little strange if you are not used to it but shortly after you feel almost a "melting" across your forehead as physical tension says "buh bye." Nasya is highly beneficial for any discomforts above the clavicles, including emotional discomforts.

Potential benefits of nasya:

- Relieves tension in the jaw, neck, head, upper spine, and shoulders
- Strengthens facial bones
- Promotes restful sleep

- Promotes clarity in the mind
- Reduces anxiety, worry and stress

NETI POT

Neti pot is a yogic tradition (not classical Ayurveda) and actually pretty common considering you can find it at local drug store chains. Neti pot is a saline or salt water rinse through the nose and used most by those who have bad allergies or a stuffy nose. It is equally important to do neti pot as a preventative measure because our noses collect everything we breathe. All the stuffs! Pollutants, smoke, chemicals, fumes, pollen, dust, stray mosquitos and other junk flying in the air go right through our nose. Over time, our nose turns into a dirty little filter. Using a neti pot cleans it out so we begin breathing clearly while inhaling good, clean prana.

Salt is warming, while the water liquifies. Excess kapha (snot) is then loosened and can escape through the opposite nostril. Fancy! It's not the most attractive therapy (for a laugh, google neti pot videos, and no, I'm not doing one), but it works and it's easy.

PANCHAKARMA

Panchakarma *(puncha-CAR-muh)* is the super deluxe mega cleanse of all Ayurvedic therapies. I cannot possibly explain it all here, there are too many parts and variables, but I'll give you an overview. Traditionally it takes three weeks to complete from start to finish. You would need to work with an Ayurvedic Doctor for this, but you should still know what it is.

The backstory. Doshas go through several stages of imbalance which are caused by weak agni, ama formation, and/or dosha aggravation/increase. We don't immediately get imbalanced, but there are subtle warning signs along the way and if we ignore them, we get further into the imbalance.

When the doshas are imbalanced badly enough they start moving from their original location and look for vulnerable tissues (different for every person) to nestle into. The doshas essentially run away from their original locations and take residence somewhere else. That, is a problem. When doshas travel where they don't belong they can cause cause pain (vata), inflammation (pitta) or swelling (kapha). The effects are not limited to these and a myriad of other imbalances can occur, too. When these doshas have gone rogue, you will notice the imbalance and discomfort. It is no longer a subtle hint — we will feel like crap.

learn

Panchakarma translates to "five actions."

Ayurvedic insiders call it "PK."

When doshas are where they don't belong they can cause cause pain (vata), inflammation (pitta) or swelling (kapha).

A Full PK: Prep-Clean-Restore. Before PK, we would eat a kitcahri mono-diet and receive daily massages to corral the imbalanced and rogue doshas back to the digestive tract. Panchakarma is the group of "five actions" that work to clean out those imbalanced doshas. The actions can be completely tailored to the individual based on their prakruti and vikruti and the imbalance that is bringing discomfort.

The five cleansing actions known as panchakarma are:

1) Vamana (VAH-mun-uh)— therapeutic vomiting, for kapha problems because the seat of kapha is in the stomach.
2) Virechana (veer-AY-chun-uh) — medicated purgation, for pitta problems because the seat of pitta is in the small intestines.
3) Basti (BUH-stee)— medicated enema, for vata problems because the seat of vata is in the colon.
4) Nasya — nasal medication because the nose is the gateway to the brain.
5) Raktamoksha (ROCK-ta-MOKE-shuh) — blood letting for pitta because pitta governs the blood.

Any one or more of these might be indicated for a person based on their current state, history, season and imbalance. Phew. That was a lot of work and we feel so tired, but we are clean! Afterwards, we rejuvenate to bring the body back to full strength. So again, a full panchakarma is a prep phase, a cleanse phase, and a rejuvenation phase.

Benefits of PK:
- Removes imbalanced doshas and maintains their balance
- Kindles agni, improves digestion, removes ama
- Strengthens weak tissues
- Sharpens sense organs
- Prevents aging
- Gives energy

It is recommended that we do PK once a year during middle age (30–60 years) as prevention, but us Westies might not be able to take off for three weeks at a time to do so. If you practice dinacharya and simple kitchari mono diet when you are feeling out of sorts, it will help prevent a lot of problems.

COMMON WESTIE PROBLEMS

Common vata problems

CONSTIPATION

Vata's main location is in the colon so one of the first signs that vata is imbalanced is constipation, bloating or gassies. Constipation can be caused by stress, not enough oils in the diet, cold and dry, frozen or stale foods, coffee, carbonated beverages and lack of regular exercise.

Balancing tips for constipation:
- Follow a vata-balancing diet.
- Eat fruits as a snack. Citrus fruits and banana are best, don't mix them.
- Soak three prunes in hot water for 5 minutes when you wake up, then eat the prunes. Have herbal teas or warm water (no food) until you poop.
- Massage warm (a must!) sesame or castor oil clockwise around the belly button, starting a the belly button and making a bigger circle each time for three circles. Repeat 10 times and then apply a hot water bottle.
- Daily yoga or walking. Yoga gives the internal organs a massage and walking is the best exercise for the large intestines.

ANXIETY/WORRY

The vata mind races into the future where they tend to play the "what if" game. They will come up with all the worse possible scenarios in any situation. This actually causes them to react (internally and externally) as if the "what if" is really happening. A surge of anxiety and panic runs through their bodies because their mind is worrying about something that does not exist! We need to pause, take a breath, look around and realize that if we stay here, we are just fine. We can't predict the future, nor does it exist yet, so why worry. Stay here, stay present.

Balancing tips for anxiety/worry:
- Use essential oils like lavender, patchouli or sandalwood on pulse points.
- Take 10 slow, deep, belly breaths through the nose.
- Lightly warm milk with a piece of saffron and raw cane sugar and sip.
- Say, "No." Don't take on too many projects.
- Daily abhyanga or rub the top of the head and bottoms of feet with warm sesame oil.
- Inverted yoga poses.
- Strength training is ideal.
- Daily so hum or alternate nostril breathing.
- Daily meditation, if even 5 minutes.

Balancing tips for insomnia pg. 82

COLD FINGERS AND TOES

Vatas are almost always cold. Keeping warm will be a constant life long practice for them especially in winter months. The goal will be to increase heat internally and externally.

Balancing tips to relieve cold:
- Do abhyanga with warm sesame oil.
- Place a space heater under your desk at work.
- Favor warm foods and drinks, nothing cold or iced.
- Rub hands together briskly for 30 seconds, creating friction inside and out!
- Take frequent breaks to move around.
- Daily exercise and sweat.
- Enjoy ginger in your foods and tea to increase heat.
- Massage warm sesame oil on fingers and toes before going outside in the cold.

DRY SKIN

Similar to the cold quality, vata will be constantly trying to manage their dry skin. Vata skin is thin and therefore dries easily, kinda like a thin patch of mud. When mud dries, it cracks, which is similar to wrinkles on our skin. Unlike mud, water is not enough to keep skin pliable, instead we need to use oils. Keep skin unctuous during all seasons to keep elasticity and prevent early wrinkles.

Balancing tips for dry skin:
- Abhyanga
- Use warm oils instead of lotion
- Eat oils, too! What happens on the inside shows up on the outside.
- Showers should not be too hot. Water that is too hot is very drying. Use the oil, then shower with warm water.
- Steam room, or steam shower. Steam up the bathroom, then turn the water temperature down for the shower.

Common pitta problems

Pitta governs the skin and especially in summer can open the door to a slew of skin problems including sunburns, rashes, heat bumps, acne and redness. In addition to cooling the skin topically, don't forget to cool your diet, emotions and stress levels! Everything that's happening on the inside shows up on the outside.

Balancing tips for pitta skin:

- Follow a cooling, grounding, pitta-balancing diet
- Omit very spicy, salty, overly greasy, extra meaty, or sour foods
- Sandalwood powder mixed with water or milk makes an instantly cooling paste for the skin (especially a red, hot face) and reducing redness. Sandalwood essential oil and soap also works.
- Aloe is cooling, astringent, and best when used topically straight from the plant. Aloe vera juice cools us from the inside out.
- So hum or deep, slow breathing from the belly (10 breaths minimum) calm stress levels
- Massage with coconut oil as full body skin moisturizer
- Blend cilantro leaves into a paste and use topically on hot skin or bug bites
- Make turmeric paste made with milk or water and apply topically to zits. Wash off (your skin will be a little yellow so don't spread it all over). Tumeric is great to put on cuts n' scrapes too!

HEARTBURN

Heart. Burn. Those two little words explain it perfectly when there is too much burn, too much heat in the bod! Foods like tomatoes, peppers, onion, garlic, alcohol, red meat, fermented foods, salt and spicy foods are all heating. Especially in hot weather and bright sun, you might find yourself with a bit of the burn.

Balancing tips for heartburn:

- Drinking cool milk.
- Licorice tea will reduces acidity. Drink daily to prevent heartburn for the long term.
- Don't overeat or eat within 3 hours of bedtime.
- Don't eat the foods that give you heartburn.
- Don't eat in between meals.
- Consumption of alcohol will make heartburn worse.

BURNING OR ITCHY EYES

Pitta also governs the eyes so any redness or itchiness can be a pitta problem Squinting, straining (computer) and wearing contact lenses for too long take their toll.

Balancing tips for burning or itchy eyes:

- Soak feet in cool water, bonus to put lavender drops in it.
- Massage feet with coconut oil or ghee.
- Place cucumber slices on closed eyes.
- Soak a cotton ball in rosewater or milk and place on closed eyes.
- Remove contact lenses in the early evening.
- Take regular breaks from the computer and look outside focusing on nature for a few minutes to reduce stress and give eyes a break.

IRRITABILITY OR ANGER

You must chill! A quick temper or feelings that your "blood is boiling" are common reactions we might have in moments of stress. The good news is that these flaming bursts don't last very long, but in these moments pittas (vatas too) might say or do something they wish they hadn't. The key is to reduce stress overall so that eventually the small irritants will just roll off your back.

Balancing tips to ease irritability:

- Bring the breath to your belly and do 10 breaths slowly and deeply
- Nadi shodhanam (p. 167)
- Daily meditation, if even 5 minutes
- Daily gratitude list of 10 things

FRUSTRATIONS WITH OTHER PEOPLES' BEHAVIOR.

Pittas, others are not going to behave, think, or strive like you will. You set a higher bar that others might not care if they match. Their goals and drivers are different than yours. Let go of that expectation and stop taking on their workload in order to complete it to your satisfaction. Instead of judging and wallowing in frustration, teach. Lead by example and show them how it's done. Take some deep breaths and humble yourself because at one point you were learning too. At one point you were daft and unrefined. At one point you were moving too quickly and missed details. You have probably even failed. At some point you have hurt someone's feelings. You are not perfect and neither are they. When you get frustrated with others, work from your heart in a space of mentorship, patience, and compassion. This is coming from a fellow pitta — I know I can be direct with you.

Common kapha problems

AMA
You know it well by now (p. 95).

DEPRESSION
Kaphas are emotionally sensitive (though they may not show it) and can slip into an emotional funk that is hard to get out of. Despite their jolly nature on the outside, they do not deal well with feelings of loss, which can plummet them into a deep, sad space. They can become weighed down with grief and their otherwise graceful and positive outlook turns dark. Contributing to depression is eating too late or eating too heavy, so their diet is crucial to their mental well being.

Balancing tips for depression:
- Clear any ama.
- Eliminate refined sugars, fried foods, soda and candy.
- Put on loud, upbeat music and dance and sing. Lively, energetic music will bring you back to center and fill you with life and happiness.
- Go for a brisk walk in nature, take deep inhales bringing in lots of prana.
- Wake up in vata time, don't sleep too late, or take naps
- Volunteer!
- Use essential oils or scents like grapefruit, ylang ylang or lemongrass
- Practice daily morning kapalabhati (p. 167). Internal heat will increase and burn off any stagnant, cob-webby thoughts.
- Wear bright colored and feminine clothes

WEIGHT GAIN
Since kaphas have low and steady agni (and enjoy the sweetie foods), they are also prone to weight gain. Kaphas may feel like it's a forever struggle, but with some new habits they will begin to feel lighter and energized!

Balancing tips for weight gain:
- Dinner should be small and light.
- Favor lots of vegetables. Veggies should take up most space on the plate.
- Favor light and dry snacks like popcorn or rice cakes.
- Eat only one large meal or two regular meals per day.
- Eliminate refined sugars, fried foods, soda and candy.
- Foods should be savory with good heat and spiciness.
- Skip dinner once a week so agni can catch up.
- Get moving by doing daily cardio exercise or kapalabhati.
- Release and forgive heavy emotions, grief, traumas, or past relationships.

exercise for letting go
Go for a walk outside and find a great little leaf. Choose one that speaks to you that you really love. Hold it on your walk and enjoy it and then, as it represents whatever you are trying to shed, let it go.

ALLERGIES

Heavy rains, moisture and pollens can cause allergies. Here are some remedies to help reduce the sneezing, wheezing and congestion.

Balancing tips for allergies:

- Use a neti pot daily (p. 207).
- Massage the sides of your nose to open sinus passages.
- Favor warm, spicy, light foods. Turmeric and ginger powder will be your best friends!
- Eliminate cold foods, especially yogurt.
- Drops of eucalyptus or camphor essential oil on the floor of your shower and inhale deeply.
- Sit in a sauna or some other warm, dry environment (like Arizona).
- Daily meditation.
- Write down your most simple pleasures, simple joys.

Note: Kaphas don't have that many imbalances. They are the healthiest of all the doshas, but the imbalances they do have will have a lasting impact and will likely take a longer time to reverse.

The most common Westie problem is tri-doshic: stress

STRESS

We live in a never-ending constant flow of busy. We work long hours, rush to eat lunch, race to meeings, race to get our work done, endure a hefty commute in traffic, live far from our families, worry about finances, shuffle to events on the weekends, and probably don't have time for proper exercise. Exhausted, we fall flat on our faces in bed at night only to do it all again the next day. Where is our reprieve? Due to lack of time and focus, we take prescriptions to help us sleep, help us lose weight, to help reduce anxiety, to help uplift depression, and the list goes on. We are not built to run constantly and over time the stress will break us down. We will suffer from burn out.

So what do we do? We use all of our Ayurvedic tools including nutrition, exercise, the senses, nature and our mind to bring us back to center.

Stress-reducing tips:

- Shift your clock to an Ayurvedic schedule.
- Take a good break for lunch, away from your desk.
- Breathe intentionally. Alternate nostril breathing or so hum.
- 5–15 minute daily meditation.
- Eliminate or limit coffee or caffeinated tea.
- Omit soda, sugary coffee drinks, sugary foods.
- Eat sattvic foods.
- Write out a daily list of 10+ things you are grateful for and why.
- Apply your favorite aromatherapy.
- Exercise for 30 minutes daily.

Practicing even one or two of these on a daily basis will make a huge difference. Notice, these tips are multi-faceted touching on a well-rounded balance for our favorite trio; mind, body, spirit. In fact, nothing we have talked about from an Ayurvedic perspective has a singluar approach or a magic bullet; everything is integrated.

doshas under stress

Vatas will become emotionally unstable whether snapping at others or having moments of irrational rage. They might feel physically weak or shaky. They might cry and feel like the world is crumbling around them.

Pittas will likely keep their stress inside and they will take on more work to keep control of the situation. If their stress comes out on the outside they might start barking orders. Physically they may experience headaches, heartburn, ulcers and frequent loose poops.

Kaphas don't get stressed easily or often. It takes a lot to stress out a kapha, but when they get to their breaking point it is a force to be reckoned with. They will become incredibly stubborn, not open to any body else's opinions until they get their work done or until the stress has passed.

book recommendations

If the Buddha Got Stuck,
by Charlotte Kasl

The Power of Full Engagement,
by Jim Loehr and Tony Schwartz

The Not So Big Life,
by Sarah Susanka

Hip Tranquil Chick,
by Kimberly Wilson

14
INTE-GREAT

Here's where it all gels

PUTTING IT ALL TOGETHER

Here we are! WOW! You have read an entire book about Ayurveda! How 'bout them apples?! Along the way you have gathered some insights about yourself and probably others too. Here's where you put them all together to make a plan for yourself.

You have learned about the foundations of Ayurveda including the elements, the doshas, nutrition, meal plans, exercise, the senses, and the mind. You may have already started making simple changes and have started to notice differences. The key is to get those awesome changes to stick — don't forget about them — and keep them as a habit.

So! *rubbing hands together* It's time to start living according to YOU. Let's bring your life to the forefront now and start to apply what you've learned.

LIFE CHECK AYURVEDIC BASIC PRACTICES

You can start by making sure you are doing these basic daily practices. You might be doing some of these things already. That's great! Check off what is already part of your routine. For the rest, choose two to work on over the course of a couple weeks or a month. Record how you feel and add more basics until you've got all ten as habits. If you simply do these things below, you will be leagues ahead in taking care of yourself!

On a daily basis do I...?

☐ Wake before sunrise (even 10 minutes counts!)
☐ Cleanse the sense organs (scrape tongue, brush teeth, clean eyes)
☐ Drink a glass of water after cleaning sense organs
☐ Poop
☐ Practice 5 minutes of pranayama (pick one, p. 165)
☐ Practice 5–10 minutes of meditation or sitting quietly, eyes closed
☐ Enjoy a small, warm breakfast, sitting down
☐ Omit coffee or adjust coffee for my dosha (p. 150), having only one cup
☐ Choose foods that balance my dosha
☐ Enjoy lunch at noon, as my biggest meal of the day
☐ Enjoy a light dinner at 6 p.m., no later than 7 p.m., sitting down
☐ Turn off all electronic screens 1 hour before bed
☐ Write a list of 10 things I am grateful for and why
☐ Bed by 10 p.m.

I am going to work these two Ayurvedic Basics into my routine:

1. _____

2. _____

To start on (date):   /   /

I will practice for _____weeks.

I will review my progress on (date):   /   /

I have noticed these positive changes:

_____

_____

_____

_____

_____

_____

YAY! I am ready to add two more Ayurvedic Basics:

1. _____

2. _____

To start on (date):   /   /

I will practice for _____weeks.

I will review my progress on (date):   /   /

I have noticed these positive changes:

_____

_____

_____

_____

_____

_____

_____

_____

Collect more good Ayurvedic habits as you go!

Once you have the basics down as good habits, you can start to build on those and incorporate some advanced practices. Some will take a longer time commitment and all will require a higher level of discipline and awareness. The benefits will be worth all the awesome work you put into it. If you've aced the basic practice, you are ready to move on to the advanced practices.

LIFE CHECK AYURVEDIC ADVANCED PRACTICES

On a regular basis do I...?

☐ Practice daily pranayama and meditation before sunrise. 15–30 minutes

☐ Do daily Abhyanga (p. 201) prior to showering

☐ Scrape the tongue (check for ama) daily before brushing

☐ Brush teeth with neem toothpaste (Ayurvedic toothpaste)

☐ Completely omit sodas and carbonated drinks

☐ Say prayer of thanks before each meal

☐ Enjoy a mostly (or all) vegetarian diet

☐ Do neti pot 1x per week

☐ Do nasya 3x per week

☐ Do a screen/media detox (no screens) for 3–5 days, 1–2 times per year

☐ Do a seasonal kitchari cleanse 3x per year during ritusandhi (p. 87)

☐ Stick to set meal schedules

☐ Adopt compassion as my "automatic" response instead of anger, frustratration, irritability, or negativity towards others.

☐ Do something nice for someone else every day

☐ Never use a microwave (microwaves destroy the qualities in our food)

I am going to work these two Advanced Practices into my routine:

1. _____

2. _____

To start on (date):   /   /

I will practice for _____ weeks.

I will review my progress on (date):   /   /

I have noticed these positive changes since practicing these things:

_____

_____

_____

_____

_____

_____

YAY! I'm PROUD of myself! I'm doin' it! I am ready to add two more and am choosing these two Advanced Practices:

1. _____

2. _____

To start on (date):   /   /

I will practice for _____ weeks.

I will review my progress on (date):   /   /

I have noticed these positive changes:

_____

_____

_____

_____

_____

_____

_____

_____

Impressive! You are now rockin' the Ayurvedic Advanced Practices like a champ. Amazing! If you are ready, would you like to try the Pure Ayurvedic Practices?

On a regular basis do I...?

☐ Practice 60–90 minutes of yoga, pranayama, 108 chants, 20–30 minute meditation before sunrise

☐ Do a scalp and sole massage with warm oil

☐ Do 15-minute Abhyanga with warm oil, let soak into all tissues for 15 minutes, shower off

☐ Incorporate all six tastes at every meal

☐ Follow all nutritional guidelines

☐ Cook all meals fresh and consume them on the same day

☐ Practice vamakukshi (lay on the right side for 20 minutes) after lunch

☐ Volunteer to assist someone else for 30–60 minutes a day

☐ A full panchakarma 1x per year

What do you notice about the pure Ayurvedic daily practices compared to the basics and advanced practices? Are they realistic for us? Do you think they are achievable based on how our lives are designed today? Some of them maybe, but most, not-so-much. The world has evolved in the 5,000 (give or take) years since Ayurveda was documented and while these pure practices worked for them back then these may not be feasible for us today. In fact, if the pure practices were the only thing we knew about Ayurveda, it would probably turn us off to Ayurveda completely.

The sweeping difference between the basics and the pure practice is exactly why I wrote this book and started **heymonicab.com** in 2008. Let's break it down and make it doable for US! The basics and advanced practices are much more realistic to fit into our world today and will still make a huge impact on enhancing your body and mind as well as extending your life. It really can be as simple as 5 minutes here, 5 minutes there, so long as we bring our mind and focus into those 5 minutes to adhere to the practice. If you were to only fold in the basics and nothing else, you would still be leagues ahead on your healthcare than you were before. It might seem too simple to work, but by now, we know that the small things can make a huge difference.

Tip of the iceberg

As we come to a close, while Ayurveda is natural, I want to reinforce that it is not light or superficial. It is a science. It runs deep and is strongly rooted in the knowledge of healers that work for decades to become true experts.

What I didn't tell you is that there are actually 15 sub doshas (five of each vata, pitta, kapha) performing different functions in our body. There are thousands of herbal combinations to be cooked in different ways, infused as liquids, turned into powders, and/or used as pastes. There are 13 srotas (channels) and 72,000 nadis (very subtle channels) that run along side those srotas. There are 108 marma points and seven chakras. Oh, and there is also jyotish, which is traditional vedic astrology. Each one of these in itself could be a book, or a volume of books.

Well, and they are. Charaka Samhita and Shushruta Sahmhita are the two foundational, classical Ayurvedic texts from thousands of years ago. The classical information from Charaka has been incorporated into this book to give you the real Ayurveda — or as close as we can get for how we live today. Again, we live very differently than they did 5,000 years ago, but the fundamentals of nature are the same.

And now the journey continues

To my fellow Ayurvedic health counselors and practitioners, let us not take Ayurveda lightly either. As Westies, we too, only know the very tip of the iceberg. Ayurveda is much more than herbs and oils. We know that much imbalance can be prevented by diet and lifestyle alone, so let's start there. We can change peoples' lives without prescribing one herb! Let us be helpful and responsible in our practices. Let us ask for help from each other and keep sharing the LIGHT of Ayurveda to reach every human on the planet who is craving it. This is our job. I LOVE this job. I am deeply humbled with gratitude to share my knowledge. Thank you to Ayurveda. Thank you to our Ayurvedic counterparts around the globe and to all the great Ayurvedic teachers.

MY TEACH SAYS, "WHEN THE HEART CHAKRA IS OPEN, WE CAN'T HELP BUT WEEP."

Share the love. Be the love.

I've wept so many times writing this book and as it comes to a close, I weep again. Welcome to my heart. I hope I've helped open yours. And in turn, I hope you open hearts of your loved ones and so many more — just by authentically being you! Pssst…you do it already without even trying, you know. You are loved just as you are and you don't need to do anything else. Can you improve? Sure! We all can and forever. So hooray for projects!

The changes you wish to make, the potential you see in yourself, the dreams that glimmer on the horizon are all yours for the taking. It all starts from the inside out. Worry about yourself first. Be the BEST, most AUTHENTIC, most HEALTHIEST YOU you can possibly be and the rest will unfold. It's all about you, baby. It really is.

Love, Monica B

Hey! I'm Monica B

I was born and raised in Milwaukee, Wisconsin — the land of beer, cheese, fried things and Packers football games. I currently work a 40-hour a week grind in San Francisco, with a two and a half hour daily commute. I come home to an endearing husband, a spritely toddler, two dogs and a cat. Despite the busyness, I make time to do daily meditation and pranayama, eat fresh foods and exercise regularly. I've also been the sole creator behind the Ayurvedic blog **heymonicab.com**, since 2008. Believe me, I know what it's like to have a full schedule and I have become an expert at tucking Ayurveda neatly into a modern life.

Please note, I am not an Ayurvedic doctor or an MD. I am not an enlightened yoga guru and I do not sit on a mountain top to meditate for weeks. I am your average, non-doctorey person, turned Ayurvedic fanatic and teacher. I am an Ayurvedic life counselor determined to educate and improve the lives of all those who crave to learn and practice Ayurveda.

I've spent my career as a graphic designer and creative staffing recruiter and am also a certified personal trainer. In 2009, I received my diploma of Ayurvedic sciences and in 2010, went to India to receive my certification in panchakarma. I bring Ayurveda wherever I go, talk about it all the time and infuse it into every part of the world that surrounds me. If I can incorporate Ayurveda into my wonky-busy schedule, you can, too.

"YOU HAVE TO BELIEVE WE ARE MAGIC.
NOTHIN' CAN STAND IN OUR WAY.
YOU HAVE TO BELIEVE WE ARE MAGIC.
DON'T LET YOUR AIM EVER STRAY.
AND IF ALL YOUR HOPES SURVIVE,
YOUR DESTINY WILL ARRIVE.
BRING ALL YOUR DREAMS ALIVE,
FOR YOU."

– MAGIC BY OLIVIA NEWTON JOHN

Monica B's must-have favorites

Favorite Books

Absolute Beauty, by Pratima Raichur. A beautiful book on Ayurveda and skincare with fun skincare recipes. My favorite Ayurvedic book.

Creative Visualization, by Shakti Gawain. This was the very first "alternative" book I ever picked up, back in 2006, when I didn't know anything about the laws of energy.

The Crossroads of Should and Must, by Elle Luna. A short inspirational book about the life we feel we should live, and the life we feel we *must* live.

The Desire Map, by Danielle LaPorte. Create "goals with soul" by tapping into how you want to feel. Your deepest desires and feelings are the seed from where the rest of life sprouts and blossoms.

Eat, Taste, Heal, by Thomas Yarema, Daniel Rhoda and Johnny Brannigan. A modern and Ayurvedic cookbook.

Hip Tranquil Chick, by Kimberly Wilson. Modern and inspirational yoga, business and lifestyle book.

If the Buddha Got Stuck, by Charlotte Kasl. Ideas on moving your life, energy, positivity in a forward direction while letting go of what does not serve you.

The Kind Diet, by Alicia Silverstone. A fun, light-hearted, non-judgey approach to eating vegan and living a vegan lifestyle.

Perfect Health for Kids, by John Douillard. Fantastic book on Ayurvedic prevention and remedies for our kiddos.

The Power of Full Engagement, by Tony Schwartz. A whole-istic perspective on balancing life and the workplace to achieve maximum efficiency.

Quantum Healing, by Deepak Chopra. Philosophies on using the mind and our energy to heal.

Write it Down, Make it Happen, by Henriette Anne Klauser. Write down your deepest desires, wishes and goals and watch them manifest.

Online Resources

Banyanbotanicals.com

Everydayayurveda.com

Heymonicab.com

Joyfulbelly.com

Lifespa.com

MAPI.com

Myayu.com

Products and Brands

AyurFoods: Tasty and balancing Ayurvedic foods

Banyan Botanicals: Ayurvedic products including herbs and massage oils

Boditonic: Fabulously luxurious sesame oils in baby scent (my fav) and original, which is lemongrassy.

Floracopeia: Great resource for Aromatherapy, nice products

Pratima Skincare: Wonderful Ayurvedic skincare products

Pure Indian Foods: My favorite grass-fed ghee

Simply Divine Botanicals: Natural skincare and beauty line. Awesome products I use all the time.

Monica B's network of Ayurvedic wellness centers & schools

Arun Deva
Los Angeles, Calif.
Teachings, Ayurvedic Clinical
Practice, Ayurvedic Yoga Therapy
Ayurvedic and Yogic Protocols,
Vedic Studies.
yogarasayana.com

The Ayurvedic Institute
Dr. Vasant Lad
Albuquerque, N.M.
Leading Ayurvedic school
and health spa since 1984
ayurveda.com

**California College
of Ayurveda (CCA)**
Grass Valley, Calif.
Ayurvedic courses and
panchakarma center
ayurvedacollege.com

The Chopra Center
Carlsbad, Calif.
Yoga, wellness, Ayurveda clinic
and spa. Full online resource.
chopra.com

**Dr. Jay's Ayurveda &
Panchakarma Center**
Dr. Jay Apte
Mountain View, Calif.
Ayurveda and
panchakarma center
hnwellness.com

Kanyakumari Ayurveda
Milwaukee, Wis.
Accredited Ayurveda and Yoga
school, full service Ayurvedic
healing center
kanyakumari.us

Kerala Ayurveda Academy
Various locations
Ayurvedic school and
wellness centers
ayurvedaacademy.com

LifeSpa
Dr. John Douillard
Boulder, Colo.
Ayurvedic teachings, clinic,
products. Full online resource.
lifespa.com

Maharishi Ayurveda
Fairfield, Iowa
Ayurvedic clinic and full
online resource.
mapi.com

Mount Madonna Institute
Watsonville, Calif.
Yoga, Ayurvedic medicine,
massage and community studies
mountmadonna.org

**Ojas Ayurvedic
Wellness Center**
Dr. Shekhar Annambhotla
Coopersberg, Pa.
Ayurvedic wellness center
ojas.us

Shubham Ayurveda
Dr. Yash Mannur
Fremont, Calif.
Ayurvedic classes, wellness
consultations, panchakarma
shubhamayurveda.com

Sivananda Yoga Ashram
Various locations
Yoga retreats and vacations,
teacher training courses.
sivananda.org

Stone and Spa
Chapel Hill, N.C.
Ayurvedic healing arts and body
work training
stoneandspa.com

Ayur-what?!

HELPFUL DEFINITIONS FOR SANSKRIT

Abhyanga *(ah-bee-YOUNG-guh)*. Full body Ayurvedic massage

Adhipati (ah-DEE-pah-TEE). A marma point in the middle of the top of our head

Agni (AHG-nee). Our digestive fire

Ama (AH-muh). Sticky, goopy, cloudy toxins in the body an mind

Ayurveda (EYE-your-vay-duh). The science or knowledge of life stemming from ancient India

Basti (BUH-stee). Oil and sometimes medicated enema

Buddhi (boo-DEE). The "wisdom" part of our mind

Dinacharya (DIN-na-CHAR-ya). The ayurvedic daily routine

Doshas (DOE-shuz). Three energies created from the five great elements

Gunas (GOO-nuhz). Qualities

Kapalabhati (Kah-PAHL-bah-tee). A type of pranayama meaning "glowing skull"

Kapha (KAH-fuh). The dosha of lubrication and structure, made of water and earth

Karnapurana (karna-POOr-nuh).An ayurvedic therapy that involves filling the ears with warm oil

Kirkatika (Kur-KAH-teeka). A marma point where the base of the skull meets the neck

Kitchari (KIT-cha-ree). Ayurveda's "healing casserole." Mix of rice, mung dahl and spices to aid digestion and clear the mind. It is the main food in panchakarma.

Marma (MAR-muh). Energy points along the srotas or channels

Nadis (NAH-deez). very subtle channels throughout the body. We have 72,000 of them.

Nadi shodhanam (NAH-dee-SHOW-da-num). A pranayama called alternate nostril breathing which brings instant calm by balancing our male and female energies

Nasya (NAHs-yuh). Dropping medicated or non medicated oil in the nose

Ojas (OH-jus). Our life's essence of vitality and immunity

Panchakarma (puncha-CAR-muh). Means "five actions." A deep, personalized Ayurvedic cleanse that gathers and expels imbalanced doshas.

Pitta (PIT-uh). The dosha of transformation, made of fire and water

Prakruti (prah-KROO-tee). Your innate balance of doshas unique to you

Pranayama (PRAH-nuh-YAHM-uh). Life breath or life breathing. Using the breath as a therapy

Rajas (RAH-jus). The quality of the mind that promotes action and dominance, attachement to the senses and ego

Raktamoksha (ROCK-ta-MOKE-shuh). Blood letting therapy used in panchakarma for pitta problems

Ritusandhi (RIT-oo-SAHN-dee). The "joint" between seasons

Sanskrit (SANS-krit). Ancient language of India in which the Ayruvedic texts are written

Sattva (SAT-vuh). The quality of the mind that promotes purity of intention and action and clarity of mind

So hum A type of pranayama meaning "I am the divine"

Srotas (SROE-tuhz). 14 physical channels that supply the body with nutrients and remove waste

Tamas (TOM-us). The quality of the mind that promotes darkness, ignorance, inertia

Trigunas (tri-GOON-uhs). The three qualities of the mind: sattva, rajas, tamas

Vaidyas VAYd-yah). An Ayurvedic doctor

Vamana (VAH-mun-uh). Therapeutic vomiting used in panchakarma for kapha problems

Vata (VAHT-uh). The dosha of movement, made of space and air

Vikruti (vih-KROO-tee). Our current imbalance state of doshas

Virechana (veer-AY-chun-uh). Therapeutic purgation used in panchakarma for pitta problems